Remembrance

Pathways to Expanded Learning

with Music and Metamusic®

by
Barbara Bullard, M.A., Communications
Alex Bennet, Ph.D., Human Systems

MQIPress
Consciousness Series
ISBN 978-1-949829-28-0

For further information on the authors and related areas of interest see:

www.dnamusic.com
www.remembrancemusic.com
www.mountainquestinstitute.com
www.monroeinstitute.org
www.Hemi-Sync.com
www.higher-music.com

"This book is completely life changing. It has single-handedly changed the way I see myself and the way I think about myself in a lot of positive ways. I will continue to refer back to it for the rest of my lie as a positive tool for inner growth. It is amazing what your brain can achieve! This book is an amazing way to get started on a better you!" -Jorgelina

"I'm glad to see that this book has been written. I have been using Metamusic since 2006 when Remembrance was given to me as a gift (see below). I have been frequently asked by my patients what's the music being played in the office as it's unlike any other they've heard. I get the true fun of introducing them to the science and technology that is Metamusic. This book will allow those seekers, who are looking to connect to this material in a way that should serve to deepen and expand their next listening. I can only wonder what new insights and journeys each person will have." -Dr. Daniel Stone

"Very inspiring book! It is a very easy read and allows you to explore all the possibilities of your mind. Recommended for anyone who wants to learn something new and become more self-aware." - Bahar

"This book is an essential guide not only for those with learning disabilities but anyone who wants to change their lives. As a Metamusic listener and also having a diagnosed learning disability in perceptual organization as an adult college student, I had to find a way to comprehend the very basic skills of math to Algebra and then to Statistics. With personal guidance from the author (and my Professor), I have benefited from the advice outlined in this book throughout my college career, and I continue to use these techniques as I work through my graduate studies program. The brain states produced by music and Metamusic continue to support optimal learning for me." -Julia

"Being able to have remembrance with me where I go couldn't be any better. This book is an easy read and can really help you focus on yourself and what you can do to make a better life or even just change your mood from negative to positive. I recommend this book to all my friends. Great read." - Maddy

"There are so many great things to say about this book … I took Barbara Bullard's interpersonal class this semester and she has truly change my life for the better. I found every chapter very insightful and informative. Barbara is an exceptional woman and I can't thank her enough for all that she has taught me." – Whitney

"Remembrance is an impressive book that has high quality of content. Learning about the power of music and how it relates to the human body was an eye opener and caused me to think about the choices in music that I make on a regular basis." -Eagle

"DISCLAIMER: My work is favorably mentioned in this book and I have a strong friendship with one of the book's authors, Barbara Bullard. I am, without hesitation, biased in favor of this work. Within it, Bennet and Bullard answer many of the questions that I have heard time and time again about using music, Metamusic® and Hemi-Sync® to enhance focus and to improve memory retention and recall. The clarity of their answers, the depth of their knowledge, the scope of their research and the emotional appeal of the gathered testimonials are excellent. This book is a superior resource." – J. S. Epperson

Original printing (as eBook): 2013
Second printing (soft cover): 2020

MQIPress
Frost, West Virginia
303 Mountain Quest Lane, Marlinton, WV 24954
United States of America
Telephone: 304-799-7267

alex@mountainquestinstitute.com
www.mountainquestinstitute.com
www.mountainquestinn.com
www.MQIPress.com
www.Myst-art.com

ISBN 978-1-949829-28-0

Appreciation

Without Bob Monroe this book would not be possible. Then there are the marvellous musicians such as J.S. Epperson and Michael Maricle, the learned sound engineers such as Mark Certo and Kevin Cowan, the staff at Monroe Products who worked tirelessly over the decades to craft these products, and all the educators and professional members of the TMI Professional Division who help inspire this on-going collaboration while discovering the magic of Metamusic®. Our thanks to Alan Carr for the stunning images you will discover throughout the text, and to Monroe Products for permission to use the *Remembrance* cover art. Special thanks to Carmen Mototo for sharing her story and learning in Appendix C, and to Ginny Ramos for her help in editing. And our loving thanks to all those who touch our lives is so many ways. We are all the better for the touching.

Table of Contents

TABLES

Preface

This book is a reality!

This work is a collaboration of souls, all those who have dreamed of, participated in or relished in the results of the powerful sounds of Metamusic.® As Barbara Bullard, the creator of *Remembrance*, has spoken at learning forums such as the The Monroe Institute Professional Division, talking about the use of music and Metamusic® in the classroom, she has been asked question after question. Which Metamusic® is best for a short attention span? Which one would you suggest when I have to learn a lot of theorems in a very short time? What can I use to enhance my creativity? Do some work better during the day and others work better at night?

You will find many of the answers in this book. But there is even more. Metamusic® does not stand alone. You will see that there is a transaction in learning between the student, the subject, attitudes and Metamusic®. While the focus is on high school and college level students, much of what is shared can be applied to all ages, all cultures and in varying situations, and music crosses the barriers of language. For every situation there is some Metamusic® to pave the way.

The first five chapters of this book relate more to important concepts about learning and the brain. Some readers may just want to surf to the magic of Hemi-Sync® and Metamusic® which is the second half of the book. Chapter 10 is a summary text in the form of a story, not too different than the reality that occurs class-after-class, group-after-group as Barbara Bullard and Alex Bennet work with people around the globe.

Both authors have been immersed in music throughout their lives, which served as a natural bridge to the use of music to facilitate learning. Barbara Bullard had become an expert on super learning and had embedded these concepts into her teaching for decades. As a former opera singer, Alex Bennet had spent two dozen years of her youth with music at the core of her life. Separately discovering Hemi-Sync® and developing their own personal passions for Metamusic®, the authors first came together in 2007 at a Professional Division seminar. It was love at first sight, and even then, this book began its long journey into becoming. Along the way several other books were birthed, but still hover in that wonderful space between thought and reality. Perhaps they will soon come to fruition.

In these great times of change, never has there been a greater need to look both within and without to find our answers. We invite you to join us on this journey.

Chapter 1

The Challenge and the Opportunity: Shifting and Amazing Times

We invite you to begin a journey of discovery into the last great frontier—the human mind/brain, regarded by many scientists as the "most complex entity in the known universe."[1] Our brain is what makes us unique from other animals on the planet, providing us the unique ability to reason, create and learn. Little wonder it's been a point of fascination covered by an aura of mystery for several centuries.

So, what's different about today? Over the past two decades focused and concentrated research has brought us into the era of the New Brain. As Dr. Richard Restak[2] describes, "We have learned so much about the human brain during the past two decades that it's fair to speak of a revolutionary change in our understanding." The era of the old brain—a remote and mysterious part of the body within the skull that was inaccessible except to specialists daring to pierce its three protective layers—is giving way to the new brain. The new brain is discoverable, and can now be depicted using sophisticated computer-driven imaging techniques such as fMRI, PET, EEG and TMS.[3] These new imaging technologies provide insights into the human mind that only a few decades ago were considered the stuff of science fiction.

When the Society of Neuroscience was first formed in 1969 it began with 500 members. Today it has grown to over 40,000. The insights from this growing field of neuroscience were so important that President George H.W. Bush and the U.S. Congress declared the 1990's onward the decade of the brain. The National Science Foundation stated:

> Research on the brain and behavior is an exploration as important as any that humans have ever undertaken; more complex than exploring new lands, more compact than exploring space, and more meaningful to our everyday lives than ever before. The Decade of the Brain offers an opportunity to concentrate on this massive research effort.[4]

This exploration continues to expand. In July 2013 President Obama created a brain initiative providing initial funding of $100 million to develop new technologies and methods to understand the human brain. "As humans we can identify galaxies light years away," President Obama said at a White House ceremony. "We can study particles smaller than an atom, but we still haven't unlocked the mystery of the three pounds of matter that sits between our ears."[5]

The study of the brain becomes even more crucial because we live in unprecedented times that require unprecedented individual expansion and growth. The explosion of information, communication speed, and networking is moving the world toward an increasingly complex state. As we move from the age of information into the age of knowledge everything moves faster, farther, and gets intertwined with other people, societies, and technology. Recognizing that the sheer magnitude of human knowledge renders its coverage by education impossible, the National Research Council conceived the goal of education as "helping students develop the intellectual tools and learning strategies"[6] to acquire the knowledge needed.

This becomes even more crucial when dealing with the Net Generation. Donald Tapscott in his book Grown Up Digital presents the findings from research on the Net Generation in a $4 million conducted between 2006 and 2008. In this they interviewed nearly 6,000 Net Geners from around the world. Their brains are being rewired, linked in increasingly with visuals and music, and there is a decreasing attention span as they attempt to multitask.[7]

Tapscott's description of the net generation brain is certainly consistent with what we are learning from neuroscience research. Several pertinent points come to mind. We now know that the brain's plasticity allows it to change throughout life, and from epigenetics (taking into account the environmental influence on genes) we've discovered we can significantly influence our learning and adaptive capability. Through aging research we know that learning can continue throughout life, as long as we exercise our minds and bodies. This means that anyone (or everyone) can learn, grow, and adapt to the changes and potentialities of our world regardless of age.

* * * * *

"We are who we are because of what we choose to learn and what we remember."

-Eric Kandel

* * * * *

We now know that brains have incredible flexibility and plasticity. As we think and feel and interact with others, billions of biological connections between brain cells are being strengthened or weakened, connected and disconnected. Our brains can change from day-to-day, and we have a lot to say about it! Further, discoveries from the realms of neuroscience suggest that "the lives we lead and the behaviour of those who care for us can alter the very chemistry of DNA".[8] Genes are not our destiny! It is the way those genes are expressed, the choices we make in our day-to-day lives, that determine who we are and what we will be! It is clear from the research from neuroscience and epigenetics that a consciousness revolution is upon us, a mind expansion and thought evolution that offers the potential for a new human being.

One of the authors of this book, a college educator for over four decades, has witnessed the awesome "plastic" ability of the brain to rewire and change outmoded habits which no longer serve the students in her classroom. It is easy to teach the young adults strategies to help them study smarter, not harder, to learn faster and have greater retention. But equally the same strategies have helped a 60 year old woman in her class used some of the keys to learning that will be revealed throughout the chapters of this book to overcome her inability to pass math, despite the fact she had flunked her math courses over 10 times before---this time she gained an A in college algebra six weeks later. Or the 62-year-old man who wanted to be a priest and passed all the tests but could not learn the required languages of Hebrew and Greek. Within 3 months using other magical keys he learned both languages and now is active in his ministry in a Houston area Hospital. You can learn at any age. Many of the stories which demonstrate neuroplasticity at any time of the life cycle will be the purview of this book. The co-author has had similar experiences, working across various cultures around the world and watching the shifts in willing minds of all ages.

There is so much published today on the problems of education and learning. There has never been a greater need for each and every person to fully engage their mind/brain to become the fullness of who they are. This, then, is the starting point for this book, which is written for the "brain users" who are intent on mining more of the "golden" possibilities that lie inherent in each of our "unique" brains. However, more brain science will be sprinkled throughout in each chapter because all the keys to learning presented herein are brain-based. This book has a more pragmatic focus with each chapter and technique based on the implications of the best that science can tell us about how the brain and learning work. It is intended to help each person who so desires keys to open the floodgates of neuroplasticity to help increase learning and to live more productive lives, at whatever age you find yourself at. Just as the forty-niners came to the frontiers of the West prospecting for gold, there is much buried treasure in each of us waiting to be mined!

Let us begin the journey.

Chapter 2

Attitudes to Ignite the Journey

Success in the ever-changing world we live in depends largely upon our capacity to learn, and understanding and developing our individual gifts fully. We cannot run on idle or empty too long or too often. Learning is a journey, not a destination, requiring continuous refuelling.

In this book you will learn of many new strategies to help your brain learn. Find the ones that work best for you, the ones that free your magical toolbox of learning. While others can communicate passion and enthusiasm for the great riches to be found in the journey of discovery, it is up to each individual to discover their personal Open Sesame and day-by-day and week-by-week unlock the doors of learning.

Each of us learns differently. As we begin our journey it is crucial to understand how we learn as well as to consider our attitudes toward learning, which can make the journey more fruitful and meaningful. Dr. Howard Gardner, an American developmental psychologist with the Harvard Graduate School of Education, Harvard University, is a pioneer in the theory of Multiple Intelligence. Gardner identified eight major intelligences (or ways of "knowing") needed for success and fulfillment in our world. These ways of knowing are linguistic, logical-mathematical, spatial perception, musical, bodily-kinaesthetic, personal intelligences (interpersonal and intrapersonal knowing), and naturalistic. These intelligences document "the extent to which students possess different kinds of minds and therefore learn, remember, perform, and understand in different ways."

Gardner asserts that while all of these ways of knowing are available to each of us, individuals differ in the strength of these intelligences and in the ways they are invoked and combined. Historically, educational systems have placed too much emphasis on the first two intelligences (linguistic and logical-mathematical). However, in the current environment, it is necessary to place increasing emphasis on the more "personal intelligences", and, because of the broad spectrum of students with different learning needs, to present learning materials in a variety of ways.

As an individual begins the discovery journey of their own personal intelligences, there are attitudes that can help uncover the wide range of learning available to that individual. These attitudes can serve as "keys to learning" and represent new mind-sets to help individuals open the door to their own mysteries.

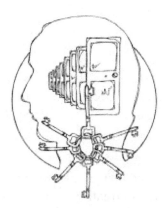

The brain---the vehicle by which individuals learn and explore the world—is at its most basic level an "electro-chemical interactive system." Brain activity is the result of the absorption of energy by neurons as they fire. The human brain has over 100 billion neurons, with each neuron having up to 10,000 connections. That's 10 to 100 times more connections in your brain than cells in your body. There's a neuronal network (patterns in the brain) for everything you have learned, every thought you have had, and every action you have taken.[10] Thoughts in the brain trigger neuronal firings (impulses) that in turn trigger chemicals which can either enhance learning or constrict it. Positive thoughts elicit positive chemistry which can open the individual to building trust in, and learning from, the surrounding world. Negative thoughts elicit negative chemistry which can limit learning, often in preparation for triggering a "flight or fight" response.

Principles of Positive Attitudes

Each of the mental attitudes described below helps an individual access more of the widespread positive neuronal net in the brain. Learning and creating knowledge is fun if you are willing to put out some effort. Understanding ourselves and the world around us is essential for personal growth as well as material and intellectual success. It is also an investment in your future.

1. Have a proactive attitude towards the importance of learning.

Own your learning and education, focusing on learning as an opportunity rather than a chore. Have you ever noticed how fast time passes when you want to be doing what you're doing? And, conversely, how dreadfully slow time passes when you feel like you *have* to do something, but don't really enjoy it! It has been demonstrated that voluntary learning—choosing to learn—not only is marked by the absence of stress, but is also characterized by the presence of a combination of brain rhythms called beta and theta waves which are present when you pay close attention to something.[12]

In addition, the same fear that causes a fight or flight response can bring about negative long-term results for learning. As Byrnes observes,

> ... excessive levels of cortisol (a substance secreted by the adrenal glands during stress reactions) causes permanent damage to several regions of the brain, including the hippocampus (important for memory) and the locusceruleus (important for selective attention).[13]

Understanding and harnessing the power of emotion can improve an individual's ability to learn. Recall the old adage: *Follow your passion.* This is the entry point to energetic learning. An in-depth treatment of energetic learning is included as Appendix A. Whenever you sit down to learn and study, it is important to create and engage a "positive attitude" which can maximize learning results and retention of what is being studied. A passion to learn or a deep passion related to the content of learning embeds strong emotional tags with what is being learned, directly impacting the number of synaptic connections created and the strength of those connections. When positive emotions create this impact, learning becomes exciting and the memory of what is learned stays with us. Memory is further enhanced when learning includes meaning and understanding of the material.

2. Have a *can-do attitude*.

Let go of past difficulties in grades, tests, or other learning experiences. Know that you can improve your learning as you begin to apply each of the strategies presented in this text.

When we have feelings of fear, the older part of the brain takes over so that we can "flee or fight." You might recall a time when you studied and studied for a test but were so afraid of the results that when you took the test your brain turned to mush and you could not remember a thing. Then, the moment you leave the classroom and release the fear, all the right answers emerge into your awareness! But it's too late. The answers were there all along in your memory banks, but fear closed off their access.

* * * * *

"Life is always an adventure, whether it is directed by love or fear. Fear is the confining of life...the 'no.' Love is the 'liberating of life...the 'yes.'"

-Leo Buscaglia

* * * * *

When we have fear of rejection, ridicule or not being good enough or smart enough, these attitudes more often than not create a paralysed state which—after a while—can lead to a condition of learned hopelessness. We can each have the **choice** to live our lives as the "cowardly lion" or to become a "wizard" like Harry Potter and find our true "magical gifts." Make your life about choice. Moving beyond your fears means choosing to take risks in order to move beyond your perceived limitations. The Carnegie Foundation for Education recently reported that the major predictor of sound mental health is an individual's willingness to risk again. It is vital to realize that growth implies moving out of our comfort zones and allowing for momentary confusion.

You can say "yes" to growth by recognizing your personal fears and memories of past failures and putting them in their proper place. They existed because you created them, but they are in the past and do not need to exist in the future. It is a truism that when an individual plays it safe, there is little opportunity for growth. As you explore the new techniques for learning described in this book, you are encouraged to take risks while keeping your focus on positive possibilities. Look upon any failure as a stepping stone to future success and personal growth. Columbus set out looking for the West Indies but discovered another continent. What seemed like an initial failure became instead the vast riches of the Americas.

* * * * *

"Education is an exploration. Part of it is exploration into the known. This takes place when we as teachers know and encourage students to pick routes into our familiar territory. Other times it is pure exploration into the unknown. Neither we, nor the student, know what the outcomes will be."

-Bob Samples, Cheryl Charles and Dick Barnhart

* * * * *

3. Have an attitude of *fun and excitement* **as you choose to learn from the wealth of information surrounding you.**

An attitude of fun and excitement ignites a cascade of positive chemistry called beta-endorphins which open avenues in the brain to learn faster. At the individual level, energetic learning is considered a state of high energy flow within the brain of an individual who is very interested, perhaps passionate, about a specific learning phenomenon, situation or process or an area or field of study; and/or energized, excited, confident, open and desirous of creating and exploring new ideas. Emotion is foundational to learning. As Johnson and Taylor explain, "The chemicals of emotion act by modifying the strength and contribution of each part of the learning cycle. Their impact is directly on the signaling systems in each affected neuron."[16]

Thus, as part of our evolving learning system, memories and the emotional tags that gauge the importance of those memories become part of an individual's everyday life. The *stronger the emotional tag*, the greater the strength of the connections and the easier to recall ... thus *emotions have priority in our stream of consciousness.*

Equally important to getting rid of fears (barriers to learning) is making certain to *minimize the feeling of boredom.* This feeling floods the brain with a cascade of neuro hormones which shut down the capacity to learn. Rather than allow a feeling of boredom, you can *consciously choose* to transfer the same excitement and eagerness you feel when you surf the Internet or interact on Facebook to your learning times. You'll learn more and retain more, and won't be so grouchy after learning or study times.

4. Look for the *relevance* to your own life of what you are learning.

Ask: How can what you are learning help you in your relationships and in solving daily problems? If you can't find direct relevance, then be creative and look at skills you are mastering while researching and learning, or even make something up. Just like the Internet, individual learning is like a web of knowledge, with each bridge building upon the past and preparing for future use.

We now know that in the minute you have spent reading this paragraph a number of synapses in your brain have changed, and the strength of some synapses and patterns of neural connections are different. We also know that the more you think about something (focus on it, reflect on it), the greater the physical change in your brain. We also know that the more connections that new patterns (thoughts, etc.) have to historical memories of significance, the easier it will be to activate those thoughts in the future. The learning experience depends on associating patterns resulting from the "interactions between the physical constructs of neuronal networks inside the brain and the reality of the concrete world."[15]

The stronger the synaptic junctions in the pattern and the more the pattern is repeated, the easier it will be to recall in the future. So, everything we learn—all information coming in through our senses—makes some connections with the past and offers potential for the future![16]

With this in mind, keep an attitude of openness to the new learning that is possible in any given moment. A closed thought such as, "Ugh! I already know how to do this..." closes the mind to new learning. As is attributed to Bruce Lee: Empty your cup. Imagine that your brain is like an internal beam of light that allows you to perceive whatever you shine that beam upon. Choose to widen the spotlight to take in more information and allow it to present a more brightly colored lens on the world about you. The brain learns easily when the topic is one of personal interest.

Learning Exercise 1

After you *Empty your cup*, imagine all the space available in that empty cup. Then, ask 100 questions to fill it up again. Repeat this process regularly through your life (once a week or once a month). The reward will be wisdom!

----

5. Have an attitude that evokes *sustained focus* on your task.

Find the best times for you to study. Some people study best right when they come home from school, and others after some break time or after dinner. Choose to make the time to learn when it is best for your brain. Create a learning space free of distractions and external noise so that your brain knows it is time to maximize learning. If you are an individual who is easily distracted, keep true to your focus during your designated study times and you will quickly build a pattern that maximizes positive results. It has also been discovered that when you are studying for a test it is often best to study right before sleep. This gives the brain time to myelinate the neurons with the new information, that is, associate new incoming information with that which you already know.

While the strategies that are discussed in the following chapters can help you maximize your study blocks, one aspect of the brain is that it cannot learn when you are fatigued. We've all had the experience of reading and cramming and all of a sudden asking, "What did I just read?" Then you reread the paragraphs and it is like reading the material for the first time. This is your brain telling you to take a break. You merely have to take a short break: get a glass of water or walk through the house. Then, when you return, your brain will be refreshed and ready to engage and retain more information.

6. Remember to keep a *positive eye* on your goal.

Another aspect of energetic learning is the conscious intent to learn. In a study of information-processing receptors on nerve cell membranes, Pert discovered that emotions were not simply derived through a feedback of the body's environmental information, but that through self-consciousness the mind can use the brain to generate "molecules of emotion" and override the system.[17] This self-conscious mind processing occurs in the prefrontal cortex (on the scale of evolution, the newly evolved organ that observes our behaviors and emotions).[18]

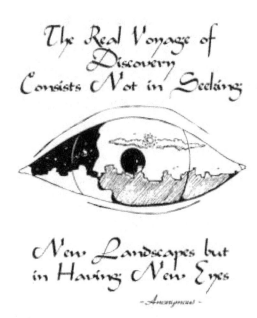

The Real Voyage of
Discovery
Consists Not in Seeing

New Landscapes but
in Having New Eyes

- Anonymous -

As you are creating better and more positive discoveries of your optimal learning styles, remember that Rome was not built in a day, or a week, or a month. There are intermediate rewards. As the process of exploring different learning paths guides learners to discover insights on their own concerning the information, learning is enhanced. As discussed earlier, this is because the brain—as a knowledge seeking organism choosing its own path—maximizes its attention and focus, thereby creating emotions and releasing chemicals that enhance neuronal activity,[19] positively reinforcing the desire to learn. Further, when an individual succeeds, there is a feeling of pride that encourages us to keep on going and push ourselves even harder to reach even greater goals.[20] Thus, the learning journey becomes a lifelong reward! Don't' get caught up in desires for instant results or the need for perfection.

Bringing It All Together

One way to bring together the principles of important attitudes towards learning is by examining *how you perceive yourself as a learner*. Approach this examination through imaginative thinking by *creating a metaphor* which demonstrates many of your current attitudes towards learning. For example, one student in a college communications class described herself in this way:

I am a piece of blank paper. I am new, unused and unsure of what I want to commit to … I could be written on with an indecisive pencil, the childness of a crayon, the bleeding vibrant strength of a marker, a simple concrete pen, or the classic mature quill. I can become a one-of-a-kind handcrafted anything. Microsoft

Words can fill my header or footer, or sadly a computer-generated so-called painting.

Although there are a number of things that can be done to a piece of paper, it can only be used once. I am wandering through school and life, absorbing as much information as I can, in hopes that something will stand out and be worth dedicating my life towards. I still have a fear that once I start on something, something better will come along---meaning I'll have to abandon everything I have accomplished thus far, finish my previous task half-heartedly to pursue the next with an optimistic vigor, or sadly stick to my decision knowing that I could have been better.

I want to be sure that the things I achieve will come together in an intricate personal way. Something I can be proud of. At the end of my life, I want to step back to see something beautiful emerging from this mess. I want to take this confusing life and work through it to find clarity, which I will then confidently write and own in INK.

The last thing anyone ever does to a piece of paper is sign their name at the bottom to claim it for their own, then submit it so someone else can judge its worth. This declares that this is MY creation, something that came out of ME, and best represented within this work. It will have no strikeouts, no correction fluid, no smudges or 7 am-I-need-coffee-to-survive-this-day stains. My signature will say, "This is what I have to offer, take it or leave item this is my final draft.

As you read through this metaphor, look again at the attitudes presented earlier that are conducive for learning. What positive attitudes do you find in this metaphor? What negative attitudes do you find? If you look closely you will discover that the author's attitude is primarily reactive with a negative bias rather than proactive with a positive bias. For this student, learning is mostly perceived as that what others external to her write on her blank paper. She has not yet found the *joy of learning* and *how important her active participation is to the goal of learning*.

In contrast, here is a metaphor from a different student, also college level:

I am like Wikipedia, filled with knowledge imparted in me by others.

Expanding my horizons with each person I meet.

They edit and reedit, create and erase.

Pull from their knowledge to pass on through me.

Wikipedia is special, in how it is formed,

By users for users, to help pass things on.

The creators had knowledge they first reported

And soon the project became peer supported.

Like so, I have been taught by parents from the start,

Then exposed to the world through other thoughts,

    teachings, writings and art.

I have many "pages"; many topics to explore,

From little facts to great books to information galore.

When something is missing someone will share,

Add to my knowledge, and make me aware.

Our goal is the same, to learn and to grow,

To freely share with the world,

Making a difference as we go.

In reading the descriptions there is a feeling of relevance and a joy of learning that comes through. These attitudes are clearly positive and proactive. There is very little sense of passivity in what this student learns, and this student is definitely *open to the transactional nature of learning* from all that is around her.

One final metaphor of learning from a college student describes more of a visual learner. As you read, note the personal involvement in the process of learning.

When I think of myself as a learner, I feel as though I am a video camera. A camera is very dynamic. There are many buttons to be pressed each pertaining to different functions/So many things to be zoomed in on.

One off the many functions is the white balance setting. The white balance button makes you see the picture/scene in the right light, see things how they really are. As I take more classes and go through more experience, I am seeing things in a different light. There is always a dark side to things as well as a bright side.

You are able to stop, pause, and rewind on a camera. You are able to pull up the menu and change different aspects about how you film. I am able to "rewind" my learning and look back to see how something that I was taught before could help me with what I am learning at that moment. I am able to change and "film over" thoughts that I've had and opinions that I have made.

I am trying to focus on what I want to do in life but in order to do so I need to pass through things that I may not want to do in order to get to my focal point…much like a zoom lens. When you are using the zoom function on a video camera, you are only focusing on the end result but I need to acknowledge the objects around it. Life is a journey of many things to learn. The objects around my focal point as well as the journey are just as important as my goal.

This student's metaphor includes all the desired attitudes of learning. As you read this metaphor, you can detect how much this student values learning. It is also clear that this student is a visual learner with a proactive and dynamic learning approach. This individual could not help but learn!

Learning Exercise 2

Now that you have read some metaphors of learning, before you progress further think about and write out a metaphor for how you see yourself as a learner. Be honest with yourself---but also let the creative juices flow. When you are finished, reflect on what you have written guided by the examples above. Try to understand yourself as a learner, identifying your learning strengths and weaknesses in terms of mental attitudes. And before you leave this exercise, think about ways you might build more learning strength in terms of positive mental attitudes.

As we continue our journey of exploration and discovery, remember to keep these mental attitudes at hand. They can illuminate your personal learning path. Remember, while it may be true that each of us is born with certain genetic and personality predispositions, the message of Epigenetics tells us that the choices we make in opening to new experiences and new growth are exceedingly important to our future success. By keeping the mind open to new experiences, we can literally wash away outdated thinking patterns which no longer serve us.[21]

Dr. Michael M. Merzenich, Professor Emeritus Neuroscientist at the University of California, San Francisco, states:

Your genes don't predestine you to be a surfer, a dreamer, a world-class chess player, a Mercedes mechanic, a Follies Bergeres girl, a drill-bit salesman or Jean-Paul Sartre. Your accumulated thoughts and actions weave neurons into the unique tapestry of your mind.[22]

Final Thoughts

Remember that each brain is unique and all brains are similar, that is, all brains have the potential for lifelong learning and developing a high level of knowledge and capability in any area that an individual chooses. Through the process of evolution the human mind was designed to learn for itself. Cave men learned via a watching and doing loop. It wasn't until the last few hundred years that the education process took on the rigidness of industrial age efficiency, herding children together in school rooms in order to turn out large numbers of individuals labeled as "educated". This process, of course, is counter to learning in terms of evolution of the species. Neither man nor machine can force an individual to remember, understand, or feel good about learning, so necessary for living and surviving in an uncertain and complex world. Learning is a very private affair, dependent upon the needs, feelings, history and expectations of the self-organizing system made up of the mind, the brain, the body, the spirit, the conscious self, and—in our example, and in our world—the eLearning system. (See Appendix A.)

Focusing on the value of energetic learning, with technology comes a natural excitement in terms of connectivity to the world, as well as its capability to support self-driven, experiential learning which is part of our evolutionary heritage. This excitement can help accelerate our journey as we continue to discover our full potential as learners, consciously engaging and embedding emotional tags and fully exploiting the beauty and complexity of our mind-brain-body-spirit combination. As technology moves into a closer partnering relationship with the human mind, anything is possible.

The question is: "What will you do with your potential?" You are the only one who can determine the answer. But while no one can learn for you, there are tools to be found to help you on the journey.

Chapter 3

The Linear Path:
The Well-Worn Road of Education

As research on the brain exploded and new techniques allowed scientists to probe areas previously restricted to the realm of speculation, no research has stimulated more interest than that of exploring the two halves of the brain. Perhaps this is because revealing that the hemispheres function differently suggests we can expand our concept of the intellectual processes.

The fascinating area of what is termed "split-brain" research began in the early 1960s when a team of surgeons at the California Institute of Technology—led by Nobel prizewinner Dr. Roger Sperry—attempted the first *commissurotomy* on a man suffering upwards of 30 epileptic seizures a day. A commissurotomy is a radical operation that involves severing the corpus callosum, a bundle of 200-250 million nerve fibers which interconnect the right and left cerebral hemispheres of the cortex. The intent of the surgery was to limit the patient's seizures to just one of the hemispheres, and then seek to re-train the seizure-free hemisphere. The results turned out better than was expected, and the team went on to perform 30 other commissurtomies. These surgeries became part of a study to determine the possible outcomes of radical intervention into the brain.[23]

As this study advanced, Sperry and his team began to notice a strange *doubling of streams of consciousness*. The surgically separated hemispheres were shown to perceive, learning and remember independently with each hemisphere cut off from the conscious experiences of the other.

For example, when angry the first patient would go for his wife's throat with his left hand (controlled by the right cerebral hemisphere) and try to save her with his right hand (controlled by the more logical left hemisphere). Another patient would unbutton her blouse with her left hand and button it back up in a prim fashion with her right hand. As these observations continued, scientists began to refer to the two halves of the brain as if they had two distinct personalities. We now know that in reality humans have two different brains in the same body and that each sees the world very differently. When a commissurotomy was performed, the *intercommunication* between the two halves of the brain was eliminated. Fortunately for the rest of us our two hemispheres are still communicating with each other. However, it is educational for us to examine many of the insights from the past 50 years of research into the different but compatible processing styles of the two cerebral hemispheres. For a complete discussion of the history of the divided brain, go to *The Master and His Emissary—The Divided Brain and the Making of the Modern World* by Iain McGilchrist.[24]

The Left Hemisphere

Let us turn first to the domain of the left hemisphere, which *controls the right side of the body* and is the main avenue of education in today's classrooms. McGilchrist says that the major difference between the left and right hemispheres is how they attend to the environment. The left hemisphere is dominant when you engage narrow, focused attention.[25] By adulthood, the left hemisphere of the brain appears to be dominant in about 90 percent of Americans.

The left hemisphere seems to process the stimuli from our environments that come in through our senses in a *linear-sequential* manner. In other words, it takes incoming information and handles it in an orderly, step-by-step, detailed and focused manner. It is evident that the domain of the left hemisphere is appropriate for much of spelling, reading, writing, and mathematics. Indeed, since the left hemisphere processes 97 percent of our words—as well as handling many of our auditory inputs—it is commonly referred to as the VERBAL brain.

Due to this emphasis on the *linear-sequential* focus, the left hemisphere prefers to process incoming information which is logical, analytical, objective, causal, and has a true-false or right-wrong context within our *cultural norms*. Because of the reliance on order and structure it processes more slowly than the right hemisphere. In both Western and Eastern cultures we often spend more time in the domain of the left-hemisphere processing style to the detriment of the creativity of more right-brained approaches. This over focus is especially true in the classroom with an over-reliance on logic and analysis and the 3 R's of reading, writing and arithmetic.

Note that the two differing processing styles of the cerebral hemispheres are separated in this chapter as an academic exercise only, that is, to facilitate understanding. The different learning strategies we can practice become clearer as we dig deeper to uncover the *aces of diamonds* laying in wait for us. The liner-sequential style of the left-brain offers the more *direct path* to enhanced learning. Because it is the VERBAL brain, we can use a process called *Semantic Realignment* to change and alter any outdated internal program that no longer serves us in our development cycle. Semantic realignment means being more conscientious and aware of the verbal programming we are inputting to our left brain. It implies eliminating the negative and destructive words we use to describe ourselves as a learner and replacing them with positive, energizing, and more life-affirming word choices. Table 3-1 provides examples of the nonproductive use of verbs that lead to negative self-talk:

TABLE 3-1: Nonproductive Use of Verbs Leading to Negative Self-talk.

I am **plus** any negative	*I am fat, I am stupid*	Refers to the essence of what we **are**
I am not **plus** a positive	*I am no longer thin, I am no longer confident*	**I am** implies permanence
I can't	*I can't dance or do math*	Becomes our **reality**
I hate	*I hate math and dancing*	Becomes a "**chore**"
I have to, should, got to	*I have to do homework* (rather than choosing)	Implies being "**pushed**"
I must have/need	*I need that car*	Makes "wants" sound like imperatives **rather** than choices we desire

As soon as you use the term "I am" the brain recognizes it as the essence of who you are. It implies "permanence." Second, since verbs and nouns receive the most energy in programming, the brain does not always understand the confusing message of a negative plus a positive such as "I am not intelligent." When used with negative self-talk a lot of neuronal energy is generated that does not strengthen the self-concept. Add in "I can't" and you are telling your brain that you see your reality one way, which can have a negative impact such as saying "I can't do well." We often hear people proclaim "I can't understand science" or "I can't have a healthy relationship." This type of self-talk can seal the fate for the person using it, for they choose to not see life beyond their "can'ts." When we realize that our word choices are a major form of electricity to the left brain, then we can understand that different word choices will have an impact on our bodies' chemistry and our ultimate emotions and behaviors.

Unfortunately, too often we prefer to take the easy road and *pretend* that we are being driven by our brains rather than taking the more proactive role of getting into the driver's seat and *choosing to create* more of our reality. It is vital that we understand we *can* change our past and habitual ways of thinking. As astrophysicist Carl Sagan states, "Habits are encoded in the brain, but they are also wired for change." Semantic Realignment is one strong approach for moving into the driver's seat. But first, some basic Driver's Education about your brain.[26]

Driver's Education

In *The Brain Book*, Peter Russell describes the incredible complexity of the brain. "It is amazing to consider that the whole of the world's telephone system is equivalent to only one gram of your brain—a piece the size of a pea." Neuroscience is still just on the fringes of understanding the inner workings of this miraculous three pounds! A popular analogy for building a simplified level of understanding is to think of the brain as a very sophisticated computer, a *biocomputer*. After all, the brain was the original working model for the inception of computer technology in the 1940's. But *this can prove misleading*. The brain is an associative processor, not a linear processor.[27] As Russell states, "unlike an electronic computer, the brain can carry on a thousand different functions, simultaneously, continually cross-referencing and integrating new information." A single brain's complexity far surpasses modern technology. In order to create a computer that can do everything that the human brain innately does, it would fill the Houston Astrodome and yet could not conceive of a single new thought that was not programmed or patterned into it! This three pounds of grey matter really is quite miraculous.[37]

As a starting point, let us conceive that *at a practical level*—just as with a computer—that *inputs determine outputs*. Then, in relation to the physical brain, *garbage in equals garbage out*. Your brain learns from what it is exposed to, believes the words you say to it, and in many ways acts much like a servo mechanism, setting about doing what the inputs (we, the individual) say we want. As Marshall Thurber and other general semanticists say, at one level language creates everything about us, therefore it is imperative that we always speak with good intent. Buckminster Fuller, one of the foremost philosophers of our time, literally stopped talking for a year because he felt it was negatively affecting his consciousness about who he was and how he perceived the world about him. No doubt Fuller would have agreed with the saying: *We become what we say we are*.[38]

* * * * *

You are today where your thoughts have brought you;
you will be tomorrow where your thoughts take you.

-James Allen, English philosopher

* * * * *

More and more it becomes clear that we need to be careful and positive about the words we are programming into our personal biocomputer. We need to see ourselves as the master programmer of ourselves. If we remember that the brain is mostly pure potential at birth and is *wired by our experiences and environment*, it is logical to look at the brain itself as the hardware portion of our biocomputer. Each of us has unique hardware. Our accumulated thoughts and learning that is the sum total of each of us now can be looked upon as the software of our biocomputer. And much like the newest PC or Mac software system can make our computers run more effectively and faster, we need to continuously update our own software through self-programming.

As you learn more about how the brain creates its outputs, you discover tools for becoming your own master programmer. As you put these tools to use, you become more able to quickly "reprogram" your thoughts and feelings in a way that can lead to more positive outcomes. This process begins by understanding that each verbal thought you process has a complementary powerful physical and psychological effect.

Let's examine this thinking process. As we have determined the brain is comprised of roughly 12 billion brain cells with trillions of possible connections to the body's nervous system. The processing of verbal thoughts and images in the cortex triggers the releases of a cascade of neurochemicals throughout the brain and body, with these chemicals then evoking emotions and behaviours. Your brain, then, can be described as an *electro-chemical interactive feedback system*.

Semantic Realignment

Turning now to the process of Semantic Realignment is a process for embedding positive, there are specific strategies that can help produce the most positive and effective outcomes. Since verbs and nouns receive the most energy in programming your brain, the first key to semantic realignment is to **use verbs which indicate action followed by *positive* qualifiers**. Positive affirmations with positive verbs are powerful. For example: I *am* intelligent. I *feel* smart. I *can do* mathematics. The term "I am" and variations on this expression allow the brain to recognize the noun as *the essence of who you are*. The words *imply permanence*.

The second key to semantic realignment is to **only use *positive nouns* in your verbiage**. Do not confuse the energy of word programming by including negatives with the positives. Competing commands interfere with the efficiency (and effectiveness) of your personal programming. Using a student as an example, if an individual proclaims, "I am not good at math, and I can't understand science," this type of self-talk can very well seal the fate for the person expressing those thoughts. The individual is *dictating their reality* and not able to see beyond some situation-dependent and temporary "can'ts." Matters are often complicated further by the expression of "hating" specific subjects when there are learning difficulties. Then every homework assignment becomes one giant chore. Further, an individual can continue to burden and slow down the possibilities by voicing and thinking messages such as "I have to," or "I should," or "I've got to" learn physics or geography (for example). These commands communicate to the brain that the world is holding a gun to your head, *forcing* you to learn rather than the individual owning the learning (which speeds up the process). While these examples were provided from the viewpoint of a student, this same way of thinking and self-talking applies across all of life's challenging situations.

* * * * *

Every negative thought I entertain in my head, which I think is my own secret place, actually strengthens the negative field that sweeps our world, unbeknownst to me—the secret negative thought is shouted from the housetops. Every time I bemoan the negative world out there that I must suffer, I have supported and contributed to it through my moaning. My secret place in my head is not so secret after all.

-Joseph Chilton Pearce, Author

* * * * *

Semantic Realignment, then, means acknowledging *when we want something* and *owning that desire*. Using any negative self-talk can make the process so much harder. Notice that when a person wants a new iPhone or iPod or even a new car, they don't sit there and waste time telling themselves they *can't* get it. They put energy into figuring out ways they *can* purchase it and when that will occur. Conversely, when you use negative self-talk your brain believes it. There is not a magician in the brain who says, "Well, we know he doesn't really believe this, so let's do what we can to make it happen and surprise him." It just doesn't work that way. Your brain believes the messages you give it, so make them positive and proactive ones. Like Henry Ford said in the 1940's, long before neuroscience had proved him right, "If you think you can or you think you can't, you're right."[39]

Learning Exercise 3

Quiet your mind for a moment and reflect on how history would change if everyone thought in negative patterns. It was once considered humanly impossible to run the mile in four minutes or less. After Roger Bannister decided he *could* run the mile in four minutes and *made it happen*, the following month 52 other men did it as well, because they knew it is was possible! For those of you old enough, remember Mark Spitz, the great swimmer of the 1976 Summer Olympics who won *six gold medals*. So many swimmers around the world wanted to be the next Mark Spitz that the competition increased from each Olympics to the next until in 2010 the incomparable Michael Phelps won *eight* gold medals. Records are made to be broken. Our brains are *made to be challenged and to achieve greater and greater goals*. Give yourself a fighting chance by telling your brain you *can* do what you choose to do. *Do this now!*

Below you will find a list of the Bummer words to eliminate from your vocabulary about yourself, and some more positive and proactive terms to replace them with. To realign your language begin to use the following words instead of any negative messages you are currently in the habit of using: *I am* (plus a positive); *I can/I do*; *I want/I choose*; *I will/desire/want*; *I hope*; *I have faith*.

* * * * *

Words, like angels, are powers which have invisible power over us.

They are personal presences which have whole mythologies ... and their own guarding, blaspheming, creating and annihilating effects.

-James Hillman, Author

* * * * *

A popular way to specifically incorporate Semantic Realignment for personal change is to craft specific affirmations designed around chosen concrete goals. Affirmations are simple written and spoken phrases that program in the desired self-fulfilling prophecy we wish to create for ourselves. Following the keys of Semantic Realignment, these affirmations should be filled with strong, positive verbs and modifiers. In his book, *Seven Habits of Highly Effective People*, Stephen Covey lists the formula for effective affirmations. As Covey says, "A good affirmation has five basic ingredients: it's personal, it's positive, it's present tense, it's visual and it's emotionally positive."

For maximum impact, another important guideline for phrasing affirmations is to be sure to have an achievable goal, then phrase the affirmation *as if the goal has already been achieved.* Because cellular changes in the body turn over 10 percent every 21 days and 25 percent every 6 weeks, most habits can be rewired in the brain in the timeframe of three to six weeks. Therefore, affirmations are most effective when broken down into six-week chunks. If your desired goal will, realistically, take a year to achieve, then break it down into smaller, more attainable goals that make it less overwhelming. For example, a goal may be to graduate from college with a perfect 4.0! Your affirmation would focus on the goal of attaining "A" grades this semester, then build semester by semester toward the ultimate goal.

Combining the Covey formula, and using a realistic 6 week goal, an affirmation for "Stacey" to become faster and more efficient with study time in a current algebra course might sound like the following:

Stacey, as you begin to study your algebra homework, you are relaxed and confident. Your mind is relaxed and ready to absorb. You are excited by all the new material you are reading and watching on the Videos. You feel like Einstein himself is feeding your head with all the knowledge you want. You do well on the tests because you can already see the A's coming to you. You absorb new ideas and materials as if they were second nature to you. You find the study of algebra exciting and stimulating. You breeze through new material, knowing that your facile mind is absorbing it very easily. The homework assignments are fascinating and you finish them quickly and easily. Algebra is your favorite subject and you are excited by each new rule and technique for solving problems. You find the homework enjoyable, like playing games.

To supercharge the impact of the brain rewiring by your affirmations, it will help to say them out loud for at least five minutes twice a day. Sing them in the shower or in your car while going to work or school. Granted, it may not be advisable to sing positive affirmations out loud in public, particularly if musical tones are not one of your strengths, but you can figure out a time to do this in private. You can also write your affirmations twenty times before going to bed each night, or write them on small cards and attach them to mirrors, refrigerator doors, or any other locations where you will see them regularly and be reminded to say them out loud throughout the day. The more you speak them, the deeper they are anchored into the brain. As one final insight, saying them in front of a mirror brings in the powerful visual part of your brain (which is detailed in the following chapter), feedback that helps assist the programming changes. The more you make conscious use of Semantic Realignment and affirmations, the faster old habits will change. Within three to six weeks you will start viewing yourself with new talents and abilities, and in an entirely new light.

To demonstrate the effectiveness in Semantic Realignment, there was a woman in one of the author's community college class who had flunked math a number of times. Paralyzed by her fear of failure, the woman had left math as the very last course to take in order to complete her degree. She could not graduate from the college until she passed this math course. After hearing about the use of self-talk and considering the concept of Semantic Realignment she wrote herself a new script, and for four weeks rehearsed it out loud in front of a mirror twice a day. For the first two weeks or so she was worried that she was deluding herself, and the self-talk techniques did not appear to be helping. But she was wise (and desperate), so she kept those thoughts to herself and just kept working the process. She verbalized that she was now an expert at math and that Einstein himself was washing out her brain at night, getting rid of past mistakes and replacing her neurons with his—neurons that fully understood math. Lo and behold, on the 22nd day as she was being tutored by her husband (who did not understand how to do a particular problem), all of a sudden Einstein's laughing face came into her inner thoughts and roared, "You know how to solve this!" A literal light of understanding exploded within her brain, and she knew how to—and did—solve the math problem. As the weeks before the final exam progressed and her confidence increased, she kept on fervently with her new programming, "She now knew math!" On the final exam she actually earned the highest grade in the class! Her husband was so proud of her achievement that he bought her a trip to Europe (and went along to keep her company). If a 60 year old with a lifetime history of math failure could rewire this roadblock, just think of the possibilities available to everyone to reprogram using self-talk!

Learning Exercise 4

Now it is time for you to examine your range of abilities as a learner and to focus on the positives while determining to change some aspects which will help your overall learning patterns. Do you see yourself as being a good reader, but need more self-discipline to achieve more? Or do you see yourself as being a reactive thinker, but you want to add in more focused and logical thinking? Take a moment and write out 20 positive qualities you possess as a learner….and then write down 4 areas you want to improve on or add to.

Now, remembering to chunk these into goals achievable within the next 3-6 weeks, for each goal write out a detail paragraph of how you would act and feel if the goal "was already achieved within you."

Now write a minimum two paragraph affirmation for each goal. Be sure to include Personal, Positive, Present tense, both Emotional and Visual.

Chapter 4

The Highway to Learning

Prior to the exciting findings emerging out of split-brain research, many people felt the right hemisphere was just there in case we needed it for backup when some brain damage occurred. This perception continued even through the early days of split brain research, with greater emphasis and respect given to the traits of the left hemisphere. The left hemisphere was clearly the domain of logic, analysis and the three R's of learning (reading, writing and arithmetic). But as split-brain research evolved, it became more and more evident that equally abundant gifts emerged from the domain of the right hemisphere.

In the previous chapter, the left cerebral hemisphere was referred to as the more direct route to our interactions with education and learning. In comparison, the right cerebral hemisphere could be referred to as a *super highway*! Most recent studies have found that the right hemisphere is longer, wider, and generally larger as well as heavier than the left. There is greater dendritic overlap which allows for greater interconnectivity as compared to the left brain.[32]

Although the processing most often occurs at the sub conscious levels of understanding, the right cerebral hemisphere processes information at speeds far greater than the left—up to 850 times faster! Further, whereas the major *processing style* of the left hemisphere revolves around linear-sequential inputs, the right hemisphere focuses more on detecting the *big picture* (the holistic-gestalt) rather than individual facts and details. An analogy would be that the right hemisphere focuses on the forest rather than the individual trees.

The right hemisphere possesses a limited amount of language, around that of a typical five-year old vocabulary. The richness of this brain revolves more around nonverbal body cues and face recognition, as well as imagery, dreams and daydreams. The right hemisphere is where most of the visual and spatial information from our internal and external environments is first processed. Therefore, it is often referred to as our VISUAL brain.

The Visual Brain

For many of us our vision is our most important sense; for roughly 50 percent of people it is the main way to process the world about us. Machines that measure our brains such as functional MRI's illustrate that visual processing involves a rather large portion of the occipital lobes towards the back of both cerebral hemispheres. Conversely, a verbal thought tends to be localized to a space about the size of a quarter located above the ear in the left hemisphere only. Vision is so crucial that upwards of 70 percent of the neurons across the cortex are devoted to vision. A really intriguing aspect of this finding is that roughly two out of three of these neurons in the cortex (the part of the brain most recently developed in the course of evolution) are not focused on external vision but *devoted to inner vision*, that is, imagination, daydreaming, dreaming, etc.

Because the neuronal connections involved in a visual thought are so many times more numerous than those involved with a verbal thought, their behavioral impact is more powerful as well. Perhaps as a race we've intuitively known this all along. Many adages indicate the truism of these new findings. For example, the sayings *A Picture is Worth a Thousand Words*, *Seeing is Believing, Believing is Seeing, and What You See Is What You Get* take on new meaning when considering the high impact of visual thoughts!

Another major difference in the processing styles of the two hemispheres of the brain is that whereas the left brain processes thoughts that are logical, analytical and objective, the domain of the right brain is on information of a more emotional, impulsive, intuitive and creative manner. Nature and nurture have wired in more than five times more connections from the older limbic brain (where much of our neurochemistry resides) into the right brain, which must then transfer and influence across the corpus callosum to produce a balanced perception. Because of its faster processing speed coupled with the emphasis on bodily and spatial balance, right hemisphere development is dominant in the areas of athletics, dance, body movement, art and music.

Coordinated physical performance of any sort necessitates the ability to integrate quickly the multitude of inputs from all that surrounds the brain and body. For example, while studying expert marksmen, Brad Hatfield of the University of Maryland discovered that right before shooting there was a shift from the left to the right hemisphere. What occurs is that the mind relaxes its analytical left brain (indicated by a slow sustained Alpha brain wave rhythm). The right brain then controls the coordination of body movements and the need for total focus. "The result is a trancelike FLOW state that many athletes, musicians and other performers report experiencing when they are intensely engages in an activity." states Hatfield.[33]

Sports psychologist Shane Murphy, a past director of sports medicine for the U.S. Olympic team, noted in *U.S. News and World Report* that, "At the level of Olympics nowadays, there's not a whole lot of difference among the athletes in terms of physical talent and training. Ultimately, it's going to come down to what's between their ears." In watching the death-defying feats of the snowboarders, acrobatic ski jumping and so forth, each progressive Olympics demonstrates that the younger Net

Generation are more and more capable of the impressive use of their right brain processing.

Many researchers have speculated as to why and how the two cerebral hemispheres became so specialized in their processing activities. It is likely that this split in the human brain could have been influenced with the onset of language. Language needs to be processed on one side of the brain; when this does not occur, an individual can be faced with learning challenges or even epileptic seizures. The good news is that most researchers concur with Peter Russell in *The Brain Book* that "The value of specialization of function is that it effectively increases our mental capacity."[34] Nature has given us two brains for the price of one and the question is: How do we each take better advantage of these dual gifts?

The Growing Need

Mining the multiple gifts and the dual streaming of abilities and talents has become increasingly relevant in the net generation that has grown up digital. The "Net Geners" are active users of media which focuses more on the talents of the right hemisphere. In *Grown Up Digital*, Don Tapscott points out that today's youth in the United States have access to 200-plus cable television networks, 5500 magazines, 10,500 radio stations, and 40 billion web pages. "These are many of the reasons that we are seeing the first case of a generation that is growing up with brains that are wired differently than those of the previous generations."[35] The brains are wired for faster programming, more visual programming, all of the aspects focused in the right hemisphere.

The over-reliance of teaching to the left-brain logic and analytical style in the past and current educational system often impedes the cultural quantum leap of this dual processing. **The 3 R's are not enough anymore**. It is becoming increasingly clear to educators that the synergistic, creative, and intuitive functions housed in the right hemisphere need greater facilitation in order to access more of the priceless potential of the human brain to facilitate enhanced learning and peak performance.

Research shows that the right brain processing abilities are more multiple and faster than those of the left brain. *Thinking outside the box* and *creative thinking* are definitely within the purview of the right brain. Albert Einstein's greatest thoughts and ideas came through first as visualizations, pictures and diagrams. Einstein is quoted as saying it was a great struggle for him to express his images into language of any sort. In fact, there is much speculation that he came up with his Theory of Relativity *because* of his innate ability to think outside the limits of language. When Einstein was exploring his inner mental realms, he would lock himself in his room for days, demanding not to be disturbed. In these inner realms he would ride his thoughts out into deep space on beams traveling at the speed of light. After days and days of flights of fancy he would come back to his current reality and begin to try and write about his discoveries.

* * * * *

Twentieth century man travels in two directions---outward to space and inward to the mind. Traveling outward he uses space craft, traveling inward he uses images... At the edges of the universe inner and outer become one.

-Mike Samuels, M.D. and Nancy Samuels

* * * * *

Just as with Einstein and many other creative scientists, the ability to visualize our past, present, and future to explore and imagine new ideas and creations is one of our greatest human assets. As we choose to become explorers of our own visions, new worlds open up that are filled with possibilities and growth in understanding. In educator Linda Verlee Williams' book, *Teaching for the Two-Sided Mind*, she stresses that the mind is the

> ... door to our inner worlds, that magical realm where the imagination creates its own realities unfettered by the limitations we encounter in the outer world. Time and space pose no problem for the mind. Within it we can travel to China at the suggestion of the word or shrink to the size of an atom to explore microscopic worlds. It can allow us to become anything that the mind can conceive of. [36]

In Chapter 3 you experienced techniques of Semantic Realignment and Self-Talk that helped actualize more of your left-brain potential. Just so, there are many excellent strategies to open up the doors or growth in the right brain. Exploring the power of your visual processing will lead you to discover that the Pictures you see of yourself as a learner are far more important than your words in determining the blueprint of who you are and who you can become! Consciously choosing and working with more positive visual images of you and your life can lead to new worlds you may only have dreamed of!

Learning Exercise 5

After moving through the text of this Learning Exercise, stop your reading, close your eyes, take three deep breaths and see if in your mind's eye you can imagine yourself traveling to any exotic place? How vivid can you make the visual experience? Can you see colors? Can you smell different odors? Do you feel any body sensations? *Make the experience as rich with imagery and sensation as you can.*

Now breath in deeply again and shift gears! Imagine that you can shrink yourself to the size of an atom. [Did you know that we are each made up of octillion atoms largely filled with empty space that our scientists call energy! The "solid" matter that makes up each of us can fit in the hand of the palm when you squeeze out all the empty space. Pretty awesome!]

Opening the doors of learning to your right brain can be much more fun than using self-talk. You get to use more of your creative nature and write exciting "home movies of the waking mind." This is a personal movie where you are the screenwriter, producer, director, star and camera person. As Adelaide Bry describes in her book *Visualization—Directing the Movies of Your Mind,*

This home movie can go anywhere in time and space and can unreel any type of material you want to view. It comes to you uncensored, direct from the recesses of your mind, and is unfailingly accurate, interesting, and meaningful.[28]

Some readers may believe you are not a "visualizer," but in truth your brain has been making mental pictures since the day you were born, and is constantly adding to your storehouse of visual memories. For example, just for a minute close your eyes and try not to think of a pink elephant with big green dots jumping on a trampoline. What happens? No doubt you had a visual image of this elephant! Word pictures can evoke the most unrealistic images. In fact, the word "imagine" means literally to *make an image.* We normally have no problems recalling the pictures from our recent past. For example, do you remember where you parked your car this morning or afternoon? What color it is? Now, turn your attention toward seeing your bedroom as you left it this morning. Was it clean or messy? Now, turn to your memories to try and imagine your best friend in tenth grade. Could you see these images in your mind's eye?

Our inner eye can also construct movies that we might desire to come true in the future. For example, imagine what it would be like for you to meet a favorite rock star? Or see yourself and a favorite person on a secluded beach in Hawaii—the sun is out, the warm gentle waves are lapping at your feet and love is in the air. Whether your images are clear as a bell, somewhat fuzzy, or even fleeting thoughts, you do have innate image-making abilities just waiting for you to spend more attention on them. So let us enter the door to the magical world of our inner movies.

* * * * *

The Real Voyage of Discovery Consists not in Seeking New Landscapes

But in Having New Eyes.

-Anonymous

* * * * *

Crafting Creative Visualizations

What follows is a step-by-step process for becoming your own visionary. Remember these are guidelines that open up limitless possibilities for applying visualization in your life!

Be in the Right Frame of Mind

Visualization works best when you are in a relaxed state. This allows you to move away from the dominance of the left brain's processing and move toward the slower *alpha brain wave rhythm* which encourages the right hemisphere to be active. It helps to be lying down with your eyes closed. Closing your eyes eliminates 70 percent of the incoming environmental information. Do not try to force the imagery—let it unfold along your general plot line, and be receptive to new and surprising images which may come up as messages from your subconscious. Remember, you cannot FORCE imagery from the right hemisphere, and trying too hard will stop the natural flow. By choosing to feel positive about your visualizations, you will enhance your physical and emotional experience.

Creative visualization is also more effective when you choose a specially designed, quiet place where you can stay in the relaxed state for at least 20 to 40 minutes at a time. For example, remember that Einstein would lock himself in his room and not even eat for days when he was exploring the universe with his mind. He found that it was crucial to limit as many distractions as possible.

Scripting Your Desires

As with any movie, it is essential to create a script designed around an exciting plot line. The plot should include a positive, self-selected goal which can be achieved within a six-week period. Make sure that your goal is a *want* versus a *should*. Visualization works best when your mind and heart are in agreement. In other words, what you choose to picture must be consistent with your values. After choosing the plot-line, you can then imagine scenes where you will see yourself actively achieving the goal.

Be creative with your images and have a positive attitude about the outcome. You are the hero or heroine in your story. Joseph Campbell discovered that the *Hero's Journey* was a theme found in stories emerging from different cultures around the world. These stories have a four-beat rhythm. There is (1) a situation (problem or opportunity), then (2) the hero or heroine puts forth effort (sometimes moving through a significant struggle) to (3) achieve a goal which brings the story to a (4) new situation (end point or positive outcome).[40]

Refining Your Script

Creative *movies-of-your-mind* help to utilize the inventive capacities of the right hemisphere. As introduced earlier, these mental pictures increase neuronal energy, proving the old saying that *a picture is worth a thousand words*.

Visualize who you were when your story begins, and who you are when your story ends. Begin refining your script by thinking of your starting situation as an evocative still photograph, as if you have taken a picture with a camera. Next, close your eyes and begin to focus the picture toward the new and better you by doing the following:

Move your image closer to you. If your image is black and white, brighten it with some color. Make the image brighter and bigger by adding more detail. Remove any "frame" you have around your picture and make the edges endless. Make your picture begin to move, adding activity, moving into the Hero's Journey. But always remember, you are in control of the pace! Try making it into a musical performance, see your movie as a television show, a live dramatic performance, or a cartoon. Dramatize the fun and excitement of achieving this goal by feeling the emotions you will experience when you have attained your goal in the "real" world. If you want to overcome a negative image, feeling or situation that is keeping your growth blocked, reverse the process. Create a picture and make it far away, black and white, fuzzy focus, framed, still motion and with no excitement or energy! This will help you de-emphasize the emotional impact of a negative image.

Other Script Tricks

The more *vivid* the image, the more you energize pathways into the brain that help you to rapidly attain your desired goal. According to Peter Russell's *The Brain Book*, experiments done on visual images and memory show that,

> When the images were vague and indistinct, recall was around 70%, which was far higher than that gained by rote repetition. But, when the images were 'seen' vividly and distinctly as if they were real, recall of learned information was around 95%![29]

The second most important element of the image other than being vivid is that it is *interactive.* As much as possible, you must see yourself as if your goal has been achieved. An interactive image has all elements working together. As an example of a vivid and interactive visualization, one college student who wanted to raise her grade in History class wrote the following script to visualize:

> Carol, as you begin to study History homework, you are relaxed and confident. Your mind is relaxed and ready to totally absorb all the knowledge like a dry sponge in a big bowl of water. You feel excited about all the fascinating new material you are reading. The pages come alive for you and are full of fun ideas and unique people from the past. You are stimulated by history and find it all so new and exciting. You feel as if you are living and experiencing the history as it is happening.

With each new chapter this student studied, she would incorporate the characters from history, see herself getting an "A" on all tests and learning history easily. It worked for her. She raised her grade from a "C" to an "A" in five weeks!

Another trick to stimulating the mental processes of the right hemisphere is that whatever you are picturing must look *fun and exciting* (note the similarity to the discussion of attitudes in Chapter 3). The flow state, which marks the use of the less dominant right hemisphere, is maintained when a state of ease and enjoyment is a main emotional component. The moment you make or see something as unexciting, a chore, or requiring discipline, the logical and detail-oriented processing of the left hemisphere takes over, diminishing the impact of your imagery.

Just as in any blockbuster movie, your script should include a lot of action-oriented words and emotional overtones. Just be sure to select words that support the picture and the goal. The word-picture you create for yourself should also be in the present tense as if you are currently experiencing the image. Your right hemisphere has the working vocabulary of about a fifth grader. So put away your Thesaurus and keep it simple but exciting. Stay away from vague, abstract qualities such as "John Doe, you have the ability to be a good speaker." Instead, create a more detailed picture such as "John Doe, as you speak to the huge crowd, your lips are flexible, your mouth is moist, your words and ideas flow easily and freely. You feel as brilliant as Shakespeare. When you finish the crowd is giving you a standing ovation." Be sure and *feel* the excitement, *see* the crowd, and *hear* the clapping hands. Experience this word picture with all of your inner senses and make it as real as you can. The more your internal picture seems real, the more effective it will be in helping you change external reality.

* * * * *

Flow is the positive aspects of human experience—joy, creativity, and the process of total involvement with life.
-Mihaly Csikszentmihalyi (1990)

* * * * *

Visualization and Role Rehearsal

Based on the research that says your nervous system does not know the difference between a vividly imaged internal event and a real external event, sports psychologists have been using a technique called *Role Rehearsal*. Visual training not only increases an athlete's confidence levels, it prepares him or her for the "real" event because it also directly affects the muscles of the body. It has been shown that when a person *imagines* an activity taking place in the body, electrical changes can be detected in the associated muscles of the body, despite the fact that the action is all in the mind. Dwight Stone, the first person to jump seven feet, says that he pictured himself clearing the desired height hundreds of times before the actual event. Then the actual jump was just one more repetition of his script.

When you are using visualization, it is important to make the internal images as vivid and as intense as you can so that you trigger neuronal firing from the right brain and allow it to expand throughout your body. For example, consider the 1988 Olympic champion diver, Greg Louganis. When he needed a perfect dive to win his second Gold medal, he became tense and misjudged the board. The world watched in horror as Louganis hit his head on the diving board. Many other athletes would have approached the final dive with a negative picture or fear of another mishap, but Louganis had been working seriously with visualization for many years. He returned to the diving platform, quieted himself on the board, saw the perfect dive in his mind, and then dove for a perfect 10! Through the mental edge that imagery gave him, he was able to overcome fear and create a place for himself in history!

Some Last Words about Visualization

It is important to create a visual landscape that is very vivid and involves as many of your five senses as possible. Since the right hemisphere is filled with inventive capabilities and is largely non-judging, let your imagination run freely with your internal movies. It is not necessary to be realistic and logical. It is more important that you have fun while *stimulating the creative genius* that resides in your right brain.

At the age of 35, a veteran was failing his chemistry class and decided to write a visual script to become a success at chemistry. He had read about a Doctor in Tiburon, California, who had freed many young people from their learning disabilities by teaching them to visualize taking out their brains at night, washing them, and then returning them cleaned and smart. So he did the same with one change. Following the brain-bath he visualized Madam Curie, plugging his brain into her brain and filling it up with all his knowledge about chemistry! His imagery worked. Within three weeks of working with this picture he passed his chemistry class with flying colors. The lesson here is not to limit yourself to just what might seem attainable and logical. Remember, there are no limitations in the universe of the right brain! You are the explorer and can draw your map anyway that works for you.

Figure 4-1 is a student's artistic representation of the different processing styles of the two hemispheres of the brain.

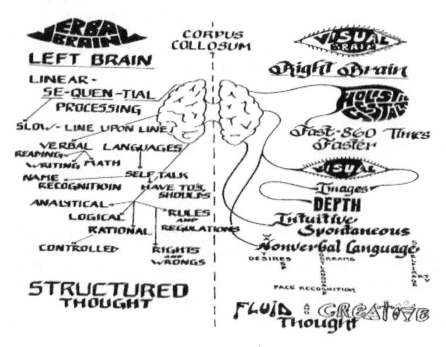

Figure 3-1: Differing processing styles of the two hemispheres.

Learning Exercise 6

Experiencing the Hemispheres

This activity will allow you to experience the different ways in which your two hemispheres process information.

Step One

Find a comfortable place to sit (do not lay down). Close your eyes and *relax* your body. Focus on your breathing, feeling yourself relax with every inhale. Feel yourself *letting go* of tension with every exhale. Do this for at least seven breaths.

Step Two

In this relaxed state, direct your eyes into your left brain. Imagine a light being turned on in the room of your left brain. Look around and see what is there. Notice the details. Now, direct your eyes into your right brain and repeat the same steps. Notice the details in this hemisphere. There should be distinct differences between what you notice in each room. Make a mental note of these differences.

Step Three

Return your attention (eyes closed) to the left brain. Imagine the letter "A" in this room. Now shift your attention to the right brain and imagine the letter "B" in this room. Go back to the left brain and imagine the letter "C." Shift again to the right brain and imagine the letter "D." Continue shifting back and forth between each hemisphere as you imagine every letter of the alphabet.

Step Four

Continue shifting between the hemispheres, only now imagine different objects of different colors. For example: LEFT—*Red Ball*, then RIGHT—*Green Triangle*, and so on. You can continue this process by imagining any variety of objects, animals, food, scenes, and so on. The purpose is to continue to notice the differences as you shift attention between hemispheres.

Step Five

Bring your attention into the left brain and imagine the first half of a figure eight. As you complete this first circle, continue following it into the right brain. You will carry this line across the middle of the brain, drawing the circle through the right brain, back to the middle of the brain and on into the left brain again. Continue making this figure eight, back and forth across the hemispheres. Feel the sensations as you link up the two hemispheres. Make at least 12 Figure Eights.

As you complete this activity, answering the following questions will help you explore your reactions:

What physical sensations did you notice during this exercise?

What were the differences in the images as you switched from side to side?

Did you find one side easier than the other to access? If so, which one and why do you believe this happened?

What changes occurred when you were using the figure eight (physical, imagery, sensory, etc.?)

Chapter 5

Whole Brain Learning:
The Expansion Bridge

In previous chapters we separated the gifts and landscapes of the left and right cerebral hemispheres of the brain as an academic exercise to enhance your basic understanding of the brain and how it learns. We introduced the value of self-talk and semantic realignment to strengthen the connections between the verbal and analytic aspects of the left hemisphere, and introduced visualization and passion as ways to open the doors to the more visual and creative realms of the right brain. However, in reality, these twin forms of consciousness inside our skulls are designed to be *connected* through an easy flow. They are joined together by the 250 million neuron bridge of the corpus callosum. We can travel the expansive highways to learning available when we awaken and unify the best of both of these worlds. When we link up these two diverse realms of "knowing" and choose to become greater than the sum of the parts, MAGIC can occur!

As more and more brain research becomes focused on the different processing styles of the two hemispheres, much more emphasis is being placed on developing and teaching *whole-brain* or connected thinking strategies. In their excellent survey of music's impact on learning (included as Appendix A), Bennet and Bennet state:

> Brain coherence is considered the orderly and harmonious connectedness between the two hemispheres of the brain, in other words, when the two hemispheres of the brain are synchronized, thus the term hemispheric synchronization. Borrowing from physics, when the brain is in a coherent state, systems are performing optimally and virtually no energy is wasted. This, then, would be considered an optimal state for learning.[30]

Think of this process as if a mirror is placed in the center of the brain. The electrical brain wave activity of one hemisphere is then reflected and matched in the other. Much research continues to explore strategies to access more of this *connected thinking* because it can increase our mental, physical and emotional effectiveness from five to ten times beyond single hemispheric thinking.[41] This accelerated process is often called *super-learning* or peak performance, something we all desire.

What are the learning advantages that occur through connected thinking patterns? According to the Brain/Mind Bulletin, whole-brain or hemispheric synchrony has been found to be a major key to the greater creativity of the geniuses of the past such as Michelangelo, Edison and Einstein. In one study of individuals who possessed genius characteristics, a large percentage of the 300 participants were left-handed or ambidextrous, a clear indication of right-brain dominance or whole-brain patterns. In other studies it has been found that the ability to switch rapidly between hemispheres—in combination with performing well on typically left brain tasks—seems to be a hallmark of higher intelligence. For example, gifted children have a more profound switching ability between hemispheres. Reconfirming the power of whole-brain learning, neuroscientist Iain McGilchrist stresses that we need to remember that all learning involves both hemispheres in dynamic interaction and we need to develop a *processing partnership* throughout our lives.[42]

Developing the Whole-Brain Partnership

How has science indicated we can most effectively develop this "processing partnership?" A first step is for each of us to become aware of which hemisphere we tend to favor in our lives, that is, aware of our preferences for decision-making, acting, and learning.

Learning Exercise 7

Write two vertical lines down a blank sheet of paper. Above the first column write "Activity/Event." Above the second column write "Logical" and above the third write "Creative." Now examine yourself honestly. Think about the different things you do during each day, the different decisions you have to make, the different responses you have to events that occur in your life. Write these down in the first column. Then reflect on each of these: In this area, are you very logical in your approach? If you are a student, ask: are you good at English, math or history? Or, are you more emotional in your approach? Do you prefer more creative activities such as art, athletics, or music? While most people will have some level of both occurring in their decision-making and actions, we all generally have a preference. Since we tend to *prefer the path of least resistance* we will gravitate towards experiences and learning activities that come more *naturally*, and in which we feel we can excel.

Once your list is made, reflect on your preferences, then continue reading this chapter.

For one of the authors, the neglected hemisphere was the right one. She did not consider herself artistic, athletic nor creative, and felt she lacked spontaneity. Since she received praise for her writing and speaking abilities and good grades rewarded her more logical and analytical style, she took only those subject in which she was "good." Although this helped her graduate with a high GPA, it definitely short-changed her early development in more creative and imaginative areas. For the other author, the neglected hemisphere was the left one. She was highly artistic—a musician and actress—as well as creative and athletic, but had to choose through hard work to develop her logic and analytical skills. Those who feel they are equally developed in both processing styles may be the lucky ones! All the better.

Recognizing your preferences, you can now begin to understand your innate brain processing styles which are your dominant processing styles. The next step is to practice incorporating the styles of your neglected or less favored style into your everyday processing and decision-making. Whatever you discovered as your dominant style, don't feel stressed about it. Just recognize that this is the right time to exercise more fully the riches of the other areas. If you are left-brain dominant, it is time to tone down the critical, analytical inner voice and enjoy more creative, full-body activities even if you are not yet good at them. Who cares if you sing off-key, use the wrong color or dance with two left feet! Your body/brain just wants to experience it all: reading, analyzing, singing, painting, and dancing. So, as the Nike ad says, "Just DO IT!" but let us add to that: "Don't judge it." **Go with your flow**. Without the influence of outside forces such as the educational system or our media-driven environment, the flow of brain dominance naturally moves every 90 minutes from one side to the other side. That is the *natural balanced flow*. It is our environments which can lead to an imbalance, which is not healthy.

Another major key to unlocking whole-brain learning is to *recognize the brain's desire for stimulation, novelty, thrills, and challenge on a daily basis*. Dr. Jerre Levy, a split-brain pioneer renown for ways of teasing forth the secrets of the whole-brain experience, stresses that the brain is built to be challenged, and that complexity and challenge promote optimal learning.[43] Much research has demonstrated how important an enriched home and preschool environment is to the developing brain. From the moment of birth the brain is absorbing and collecting information and being impressed by whatever environment surrounds the infant. Given the choice, a six-month-old brain will always look first at a *new* toy or input. Only then will the infant return to that toy or picture it has viewed previously.

When there's not enough that is of interest going on about you to spark curiosity, then your attention often diverts to the path of least resistance, and an attitude of boredom can set in. Boredom has been shown to shut down memory retention, whereas challenge and paying attention (through interest) has been shown to build good memory streams. To help prevent the numbing effects of boredom, one approach to the acceleration of learning is to seek out novelty experiences. Novelty wakes up our brains; that which we find intriguing we learn faster. The rewiring aspects of our multimedia-based culture is installing an even greater need for variety and novelty in the Net Generation. Considering the rapid change of stimuli in media such as You Tube, Facebook and Twitter, the media at each ensuing generation of viewers plays more heavily on arousing adrenaline and emotions to keep the attention of the viewer on the media. Everything on television and the Internet is so much faster and more stimulating now. All mass media know and apply McLuhan's famous axiom (roughly phrased) "He who rules the eyeballs, rules the mind."

To find the major avenue to naturally synchronize the hemispheres, one needs only to look around at the current generation, each plugged into the music of their IPods and any other new media toy available. That major avenue is music … a great variety of every style, such that it doesn't repeat often. These Net Geners are continuously stimulating their full brain through the power of music. For this generation, Stanford researcher Avram Goldstein who was one of the discoverers of endorphins found that music registered the highest thrill factor rating when measuring the brain's physical indicators of excitement—up to 96 percent! To put this into context, compare this to the 70 percent rating for sex.

Along with the endorphin/adrenaline production capability of music, brain imaging of the major portions of the triune brain have found that it is the complex stimulus of music that naturally creates whole-brain stimulation. The lyrics, beat, rhythm, scales and mathematics of music are processed by the left hemisphere of the brain while the pitch, melody, harmony, creativity, balance, emotions and poetry of the music are processed by the right hemisphere.[44]

Music also has a tremendous impact on the entire body and brain. Dr. David Tame, author of *The Secret Power of Music*, notes that there is scarcely a single function of the body and brain that cannot be affected by Musical tones.[45] Because the roots of the auditory nerves are more widely distributed throughout the brain and therefore possess more extensive connections than those of any other nerves in the body, music has been found to positively affect body metabolism, digestion, circulation, blood pressure, blood cholesterol levels, breathing rates, release of stress and muscular energy. All in all, being exposed to the right kind of music can be an all-around health tonic. The largely healthy impact of music can be intuited from the fact that orchestral conductors, who spend a large part of their waking hours exposed to classical and harmonic music, live longer than most other professionals. Dr. John Diamond, author of *Your Body Doesn't Lie*, notes that at the age of seventy, 50 percent of American men are deceased yet 80 percent of all orchestral conductors are not only alive, but active and still working![46]

Of course, not all music that we listen to is healthy or uplifting. Some sounds are actually disruptive to the brain and body. Sound therapist and neuroscientist Dr. Alfred Tomatis cautions that while music is a primary stimulus to our brains and can be used

> ...to charge the brain, enhance memory and nourish the mind, ...what the youth of today are looking for is too much of their brain. The trouble is that they are not taken up with charging (healthy) sounds, but more with discharging sounds. In the music they play, there are few to no high harmonics. The more they play their music, the more tired they may feel, and the more they are obliged to increase the intensity of their music.[47]

Tomatis makes the sad reflection that many of the young people are using so much intensity and bass in their music—directly tuning their brains through their iPods—that they are slowly becoming deaf.

The *right* kind of music has been found to be an invaluable aid to whole-brain learning states, even to enhanced state of retention that have been titled super-learning. The research of therapists such as Ostrander, Schroeder and Tomatis have helped discover the most beneficial types of music to open wide the doors of learning. They most often recommend classical Baroque music. In their adagio and largo selections, Baroque artists such as Vivaldi, Handel and Bach generally feature high-frequency compositions for string instruments such as violin, harpsichord, mandolin, and piano. Baroque has two main effects on the brain and body. First, it naturally stimulates an active whole-brain state. Second, it incorporates a rhythm of 60 beats per minute with which the listener's heart will harmonize within ten minutes of listening. This is a normal, *resting heart rate state*. The books *Superlearning: The Revolution,* and *Superlearning 2000* by Ostrander and Schroeder are filled to overflowing with research on how the style of Baroque music aids super-learning states.

This is not new information. Madison Avenue and Hollywood clearly know the prime importance of a musical backdrop for advertisements and media. It is clear that the student of today is bombarded with music everywhere in their lives except for school. Interesting! A practitioner of super-learning in the college classroom,

Bullard found that students in the 90's to the present who were repeat users of Baroque music for learning complained that this music took them into a too relaxed state—similar to when they watch television. These students no longer found Baroque music conducive to super-learning. After much experimentation with different styles of musical formats, Bullard determined that a more effective musical background for these students was to use a soundtrack from their favorite movie, ensuring it was a movie that was emotionally uplifting where the theme was to triumph over hardship.

There are specific soundtrack features that support learning. These include:

A. **No lyrics**. The left brain can only concentrate on one verbal message at a time. Given the choice of learning material or the lyrics, the mind/brain will too often focus on the lyrics, thus defeating your learning purpose. Lyrics demand too much processing attention from the left brain, and the desired synchronized state can be broken.

B. **30-40 minutes of uninterrupted music featuring a repeatable refrain**. All composers incorporate repeatable refrains in their soundtracks to influence the emotions and entrain the viewer. This translates over to keeping the brain stimulating for super-learning states.

C. **Positive musical emphasis** to better elicit positive neuro hormones. This means no musical soundtracks from horror-based movies such as *A Nightmare on Elm Street* or *Daybreakers*.

D. Musical formats must be **harmonic and rhythmic**; therefore, impressionistic jazz cannot be used for super-learning states.

E. Musical formats must help the listener stay **more energized and not too relaxed**. For enhanced learning, the musical format should help the brain stay in a synchronized Beta brainwave rhythm, and not drift off to daydreaming or diffused thinking. Although it is conducive to other states of consciousness, this is why electronic trance *music should generally not be used* for super-learning.

Find **musical formats which work best for you and your brain**. It must feel uplifting, relaxing and energizing to YOU! Studies by Valerie Stratton Ph.D, at Pennsylvania State University show that the most important relaxation factor is a liking for the music.[48]

Favorite movie soundtracks included *Avatar, Rocky, Lord of the Rings, Raiders of the Lost Ark, Harry Potter, Braveheart, Star Wars,* and *Star Trek*.

Now that we are clear about the specific types of music to use for *superlearning* in a whole-brain state, what other applications can we use? Have you ever noticed that when an *oldie* comes onto the radio, even if you have not heard the lyrics to the song in years, after the first few beats on the radio you easily begin to remember the words and begin to sing along. Soon thereafter, you may find yourself remembering what you were doing when you last heard this song. Recall of music can evoke some old memories of a relationship—joy, hurt, or anger, depending on the relationship.

Learning Exercise 8

Think back to your kindergarten or early grammar school years, and sing the ABC's or other childhood ditties. You will find they come back to you as if it were yesterday. As new thoughts and tunes come into your mind, follow your associations. This is the same way your mind/brain is remembering today.

This phenomenon points out an important way we can use the power of music to aid in memory and recall. Information and emotions that are experienced while listening to music in a repetitive way can be retrieved at a later date if the same music is listened to again—even decades later!

Learning and Memory Aids

While we've talked about how music and other whole-brain techniques can aid learning and memory, it may be beneficial to walk through that process. Note that each individual learns differently. The process described below may need to be tweaked or adapted to your specific mode of learning. Nonetheless, it can serve as a starting point.

When sitting down to study or to learn a new skill, **select your favorite soundtrack or preferred Baroque music**. Put the music on at a barely audible level so it serves as *sonic wallpaper*. Be careful to match the music to the emotional state that best benefits what you are learning. For example, if you are working on something that seems difficult and you want to feel you can *triumph over all odds*, you might play the soundtrack from *Rocky* or *Braveheart*. Play the *same* musical format 30-40 minutes each time you work on a *particular subject or skill*. This repetition of the music serves as a neuronal trigger that connects the subject you are learning to a *widely connected neuronal net* in the whole-brain. This neuronal net will get retriggered whenever you hear this particular soundtrack, just as when you hear the *oldies*.

Now **experience some slow breathing** to the count of 4. Close off one nostril with your right thumb and slowly breathe in (1-2-3-4) and out (1-2-3-4) through the other nostril. Repeat this four times. Now reverse the process with the other nostril. This can be extra effective in *lighting up* one hemisphere or the other. For example, a student who is studying math might wish to begin breathing in with your right nostril open (connected to the left brain) and your left nostril closed off. Alternatively, an individual involved in an art experience might wish to begin by closing off the right nostril to breathe deeply into the left, thereby triggering the right hemisphere.

As an interesting fact, the sense of smell is both contra-lateral and ipsilateral, which means it goes into both brains equally. The yogic traditions have long taught that to live well certain things must be done while breathing through one nostril or the other. In the last decade, scientists at the University of California at San Diego and at The Salk Institute of Biological Sciences have verified this ancient teaching. We now know that humans have 90-minute to 2-hour cycles when one nostril is dominant over the other, reflective of the natural shifting of hemispheres. When you are breathing through the left nostril your right brain is dominant; when you are breathing through the right nostril the left hemisphere dominates.

Because the sense of smell and memory are directly linked through the hippocampus of the brain, it is good to **have a distinct aroma in your study space**. You can light a scented candle which has the aroma of lemon, or orange or lavender. Pick any scent that is pleasing to you. This will aid further in the ability to recall the material.

When you have relaxed and centered yourself through the breath, add in the **positive self-talk** discussed in Chapter 3. Affirm that you are smart and knowledgeable about this particular subject. Tell yourself how *easy* and *worthwhile* this subject is for you to learn because you are an "A" student and you *enjoy* learning this subject. Remember that it is important for optimal learning that you feel good about yourself, your abilities, and your subject before you begin to study so that it opens up your brain to accept the learning. If you are not yet fully convinced about this, *fake it till you make it.* Move into a memory (a vivid vision) of the last (or an important) time you successfully aced a test. Recapture the rush of adrenaline and the positive feelings from your past *peak performance*. Connect this vision and feeling with your positive self-talk. Re-energize that feeling of TOTAL CONFIDENCE in yourself, and begin to study.

Remember to **take a short break when the soundtrack ends** after 30-40 minutes. Get a glass of water or whatever you drink, and use that to connect taste with your learning. Then return to your study space and begin again with the

Music + confident attitude + breath + smell + taste.

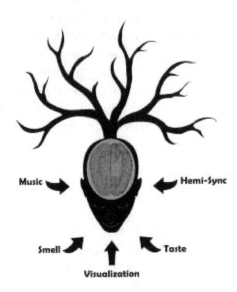

Whenever possible, do not disrupt your sleeping time by studying all night. New information is consolidated by the brain during the REM dream stages during a night of restful sleep. A good night's sleep is vitally important for full retention. NOTE: It is sad, but true, that if you go to a party or drink after studying, then it reduces your retention of the studied material.

The Day of Recall

Finally, on the day of the test or challenge, when you need to recall what you have learned, remember to quickly incorporate the whole brain techniques. As a quick summary:

Breathe through the correct nostril to the count of 4 times 4 (1-2-3-4 in and out four times).

Allow the **attitude and feelings of total confidence** in your abilities to refill your body/mind. Remember that an attitude of fear or anxiety tends to send out neurotransmitters that can shut down the recall of information. Sustain the attitudes of faith and confidence which will open up the files of memory for faster recall.

Imagine your eventual success, and SMILE, which has been shown to send out endorphines to aid greater recall.

Recall the smells, the taste and the musical format you used when studying.

With confidence and ease take the test or the challenge knowing you will be successful.

If you do happen to blank out on any questions, all you have to do is breathe in to the count of 4, allow your favorite melody of the music to flow through your awareness, and any information you studied will come back to recall in about 40 seconds.

This wonderful whole-brain approach to super-learning does not take the place of study time. It just maximizes the outcome of your study time. You study **smarter,** not **harder**. If you don't' want to study, then try prayer! Following is an exercise to do at night to awaken the Super-learner in YOU! Use your favorite soundtrack from the Harry Potter movie series.

Learning Exercise 9

Super-Learning Exercise

This activity is designed to help you understand your potential by exploring the greater capabilities of your brain.

Find yourself a comfortable spot, sit or lie down, close your eyes and relax. Begin to focus on your breathing patterns. With every inhale think "RELAX." With every exhale think "LET GO."

When the body is deeply relaxed, you can enter the domain of the *mind's eye* where whatever you vividly see, hear, feel, taste, or smell becomes reality for the brain and the nervous system.

Visualize the sequence of events, feelings and sensory experiences that are detailed under Super-Learning Visualization below. You can pre-record this in your own voice for ease of listening or you can use a precording.[49]

When you are alert again following this visualization process, sit up with a smile on your lips, and welcome back a better and more capable you

----

Super-Learning Visualization

In your mind's eye, *see yourself walking along a pathway. The sun is brightly shining above and there are soft, white, puffy clouds in the skies. The birds are singing as they soar through the skies. You feel comfortable and at peace with yourself and with the world about you. Look around and see what trees, flowers or scenery surround this very peaceful path you are walking on. Remember to see the scenery in vivid color and detail.*

While you are walking along this pathway, think about yourself as a learner. Gently allow all the many positives that you possess as a learner flow through your mind. As you allow your many positives to flow through your awareness, you become aware of four attributes that if you added these to your repertoire of abilities you could become an even better learner—a **SUPER LEARNER.** *Perhaps they may be increased self-discipline, increased self-confidence, math abilities, better recall, greater comprehension, whatever you could possibly need.*

Make the mental decision that, if you found a way to incorporate these desired abilities within you, you would make the commitment to do so. As you make this commitment, ahead on the right-hand side of your path, see a big red schoolhouse. See the steeple on the top and hear the school bells ringing a welcome for you. As you approach the schoolhouse, you feel the enthusiasm and joy of learning that a four-year-old child has. You recall when learning was fun and easy for you!

Place your hand on the door knob and enter the schoolhouse. Inside you see a brightly lit and cheerful classroom. On the shelves that surround the classroom are beautiful glass containers with colorful crystallized sugar inside them. Written on the outside of each glass container is a word. For example, on one you see, **Joy of Learning**, *on another you see* **Good Study Skills**, *or* **Perfect Recall**, *or* **Ability to Easily Memorize**.

As you are reading all the labels, you are approached by a teacher, and you feel like a little kid again, only you know this is a master teacher, one who inspires their students and is fun to learn from. As he or she smiles at you, hear this teacher tell you that you have found your way to the **MAGICAL SCHOOLHOUSE.** *Because you have found your way here, you may choose any four of the glass containers that line the shelves of the schoolroom. He or she can then blend them into an* **ELIXIR OF CHANGE** *for you to drink. Give yourself sufficient time to choose from all of the learning capabilities. Make your favorite four choices and take them with you to the teacher's desk. Watch as the teacher takes the four glass containers and pours the multi-colored sugar crystals into a blender on the desk. Watch as crushed ice is added into the blender and turned on. See the swirling kaleidoscope of colors blending together. Within this elixir are the desired ingredients for change which you chose from the shelves. Watch as the master teacher pours the elixir of change into a goblet and hands it to you.*

If you truly desire these qualities within you then slowly sip the savory liquid. This elixir has a fragrant taste that is especially pleasing to you. Focus on that taste so you fully anchor it in your memory. Feel the coolness of the liquid as it slowly moves across your lips ... across your tongue ... down your throat and into your stomach for digestion. Carefully sip every drop of the elixir and follow the sensations as the liquid makes it journey from the glass to the lips and down through the throat to the stomach. As all of the elixir is now in your stomach, shift all of your attention here and feel the sensations of energy begin to circulate as the stomach juices slowly digest all the ingredients of change in you.

Now feel the electricity begin to slowly move throughout your entire nervous system as the blood begins to distribute all the ingredients for change throughout your entire body. You will probably feel tingling sensations, heat or cold, as the ingredients move throughout the various parts of your body. Feel a total shift in the body as the ingredients move into your brain and become a total catalyst for change. Know and feel that these four qualities are now within you waiting to be actualized by your external behaviours. You are surprised, but excited by how easily change can occur when you imagine it.

Now express your appreciation to the master teacher for combining the elixir. Hear this person tell you that you can return at any time that you choose to add in other qualities or to refresh the ones you chose today. After thanking the master teacher, turn again towards the door to the schoolhouse and open the door. Walk outside into the bright sunlight. Walking back up the pathway, you feel the lightness of your step, the enthusiasm in your body for learning, and you know for certain that you will be able to fully actualize all of these new capabilities and become the Super Student you have desired to be.

When you are ready to return from your waking daydream, see a puffy white cloud of light standing on your pathway. See yourself walking into the cloud of light and then you begin to increase the depth of your breathing. Breathe at least seven times, mentally telling yourself to re-energize with each deep inhale and to revitalize with each exhale. Slowly stretch your muscles back to an alert state before you open your eyes.

Welcome back to a better and more capable you!

Chapter 6

The Emergence of Metamusic®

Nestled in the verdant Blue Ridge Mountains is The Monroe Institute (TMI), an institute created by Robert Monroe dedicated to expanding human potential particularly by using sound in the brain. Robert Monroe's journey began in 1956 when he retired from a broadcasting career as owner of dozens radio and television stations and producer of 28 radio shows per month. His "retirement" began by setting up a research and development division to study the effects of various sound patterns on human consciousness, including the feasibility of learning during sleep.

Ever the pragmatic business leader, Monroe and a growing group of fellow researchers began to work on methods of producing and controlling forms of consciousness in a laboratory setting. This research led to the development of a non-invasive and easy-to-use audio/guidance technology known as Hemispheric Synchronization, or Hemi-Sync®.

The main focus was sound on the brain. Monroe's personal experiences involving deep-diving into his subconscious were always preceded by a high pitch tone. While a lot of other research groups were already doing visualizations, guided imagery and self-hypnosis for consciousness exploration, the focus of TMI was to expand these modes and include audio waves to facilitate learning at deeper brain states.[50]

A film has been recently produced (*The Path: Beyond the Physical*) that chronicles much of the history and development of Hemi-Sync®.[51]

Introducing Hemispheric Synchronization

Hemispheric synchronization is the use of sound coupled with a binaural beat to bring both hemispheres of the brain into unison.[52] Binaural beats were identified in 1839 by H.W. Dove, a German experimenter. In the human mind, binaural beats are detected with carrier tones (audio tones of slightly different frequencies, one to each ear) below approximately 1500 Hz.[53] The mind perceives the frequency differences of the sound coming into each ear, mixing the two sounds to produce a fluctuating rhythm and thereby creating a beat or difference frequency. Because each side of the body sends signals to the opposite hemisphere of the brain, both hemispheres must work together to "hear" the difference frequency.[54]

This perceived rhythm originates in the brainstem[55] and is neurologically routed to the reticular formation,[56] then moving to the cortex where it can be measured as a frequency-following response.[57] This inter-hemispheric communication is the setting for brain-wave coherence, which facilitates whole-brain cognition,[58] that is, an integration of left- and right-brain functioning.[59]

The following visual sequence (with accompanying verbal descriptors) as prepared by Skip Atwater, the head of research for TMI for many years.

In addition to verbal instructions, this auditory-guidance process involves carefully constructed blends and sequences of stereo sound patterns designed to evoke beneficial brainwave states.

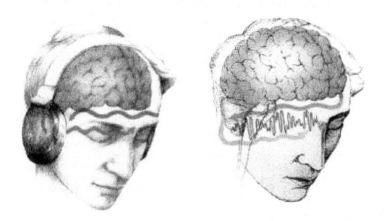

(Left) The sensation of auditory binaural beats occurs when two coherent sounds of nearly similar frequencies are presented one to each ear with stereo headphones or speakers. (Right) The brain integrates the two signals, producing a sensation of a third sound called the binaural beat.

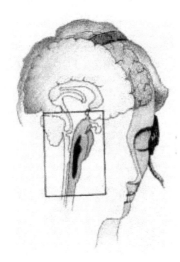

Binaural beats originate in the brainstem's superior olivary nucleus, the site of contralateral integration of auditory input.

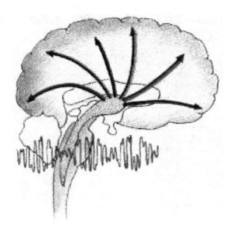

The binaural beat is neurologically conveyed to the reticular formation which uses neurotransmitters to initiate changes in brain-wave activity.

Right and left auditory input is combined in the brainstem's superior olivary nucleus and routed to the reticular formation that, in turn, initiates changes in neurological activity in the thalmus and cortex.

What can occur during hemispheric synchronization is a physiologically reduced state of arousal while maintaining conscious awareness,[60] and the capacity to reach the unconscious creative state described above through the window of consciousness.

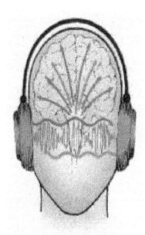

In 1971 Robert Monroe—arguably the leading pioneer of achieving learning through expanded forms of consciousness—developed audiotapes with specific beat frequencies which create synchronized rhythmic patterns of concentration called Hemi-Sync®. Repeated experiments occurred with individual brain activity observed. At this intersection, the following correlations between brain waves and consciousness were used: **Alpha waves** (approximately 8-13 Hz) and unfocused alertness; **Theta waves** (approximately 4-8 Hz) and a deep relaxation; and **Delta waves** (approximately 0.5-4 Hz) and deep sleep. While Robert Monroe initially experimented on himself and approached his research quietly, he soon began to attract other consciousness explorers. Many were able to replicate the states experienced by Robert Monroe using the sounds that were now known as Hemi-Sync®.

Opening the Gateway

In 1974, the original research group was expanded to become The Monroe Institute, an organization dedicated to conducting seminars in the control and exploration of human consciousness. Much has been written about the beginnings of The Monroe Institute in Robert Monroe's best-selling book *Journeys Out the Body*, first published in 1971. Because of the continued success of this book, many people began to come to the Institute searching for the expanded experiences mentioned in the book. Thus, was created a six-day intensive program called the Gateway Voyage, the experience for which The Monroe Institute is best known.

The Gateway Voyage was about learning an inner path based on sound. As an early participant observed, "If I had never meditated, this experience would have taken me to states of consciousness normally not reached until you have meditated regularly for about six years." He went on to say that Robert Monroe's goal was *not to give people answers, but to provide them tools to discover their own answers.*[61] An early graduate summed up about her Gateway experience,

> We all came away with a piece of some kind of special magic. For some of us it was an awakening, for others an affirmation. But we all learned that the true journey out begins within. Some of us learned to love, some of us fell in love, and some of us learned that the love we sought was no further than ourselves.[62]

In the late 1970's Robert Monroe released a series called Mind Food®, individual CDS that provide the Hemi-Sync® experience and benefits while largely listening to verbal guidance. A decade later on-going development led to Human Plus®, an advanced series focusing on embedding internal commands within the self. By 1993 over 7,000 people had experienced the evolving Gateway program and many others had been exposed to the Mind Food® and Human Plus® tools. Today hundreds of thousands have experienced the deep journey into self, facilitated through Hemi-Sync®.

Building a Learning Community

Starting in those early years, Monroe interacted with many researchers and professionals from multi-disciplines who touched areas of consciousness studies. While the instruments were not yet available that could measure brain wave activity, extensive research was conducted based on behavioral models and body responses to specific combinations of frequencies. For example, the body responses of an artist at work or a monk who was meditating were correlated with specific sound combinations. What was profound was a consistency across these correlations. As the value of Hemi-Sync® was recognized as repeatable, and new combinations of sounds were emerging for future exploration, a number of professionals became deeply involved with furthering this research across disciplines. In 1987 the first Professional Division was formally formed with members representing doctors, psychologists, neuroscientists, teachers and therapists and healers. By 1989 there were 45 active members.

* * * * *

Metamusic® is designer music, designed to create specific connected states through music.

-Barbara Bullard

* * * * *

The main topic of this work, Metamusic®, was birthed between the collaboration of Robert Monroe with one of the Professional Division members. In 1990 when Dr. Suzanne Morris, an internationally-known speech and language pathologist, asked Robert Monroe to embed Hemi-Sync® binaural beat technology in experimental music from *Comfort Zone* by Steven Halpern, a musician already famous for his work. The addition of artist-designed music with the Hemi-Sync® frequencies created a prototype used by Morris in her work treating children with a wide range of developmental disabilities. When the anecdotal video representing this work was presented to the Professional Division, members of the audience were awed when witnessing the impact of Metamusic® on an autistic child who could not tolerate touch. Within minutes of listening to Metamusic® (that is, music embedded with Hemi-Sync® frequency following responses), the child moved toward the source of the music, wrapping her arms around the boom box and allowing herself to be gently massaged by Dr. Morris while the music played. Relaxation music without Hemi-Sync® had no effect on the child. These dramatic images exemplified the power of designer music that was termed Metamusic® (meaning "more than music") to the Professional Division. Dr. Morris has done much leading-edge research during the last decades, which can be found on her website.[63]

The Artist Series of Metamusic®

It 1992 the Artist Series of Metamusic® was introduced with the titles: *Inner Journey* (by Mohammad Sadigh), *Sleeping Through the Rain* (by Matthew Sigmond and Julie Anderson), and *Cloudscapes* (by Ray Dretske). The musical pieces represented in these works were the product of professional musicians. Embedded in *Inner Journey* were frequency following responses representative of those responses produced by 18-year meditators. Embedded under *Sleeping in the Rain* was the lab-researched frequency following response of the REM (Rapid Eye Movement) sleep state. Embedded in *Cloudscapes* was the lab-researched frequency following response of deep relaxation.

As they experienced each of these Metamusic® pieces, most of the professional members felt the powerful effects themselves, and took these pieces back to use in their professional work. During this time period one of the authors wrote a paper regarding her own epiphany with the use of Metamusic®. See Appendix D. Other professional members were discovering amazing results as well.

For example, upon returning home one educator received another lesson in application of the magic that lay hidden in Metamusic®. One of her students, Aaron, was dying of AIDS-related complications. Aaron was already a user of the Hemi-Sync® Human Plus series. The educator took *Inner Journey*, *Sleeping through the*

Rain and *Cloudscapes* to the hospital and left them with Aaron's mother, instructing her to put on the music whenever Aaron needed sleep or relief from pain.

Days later, during the educator's second visit, she was greeted by a nurse who asked where to purchase the "miracle music" for the hospice wing. The nurse said that as long as the music was being played, Aaron needed no morphine. The educator went into Aaron's room and received personal confirmation that Metamusic® is more than music. As she was talking to Aaron, the music suddenly ended. Within five minutes, she could visually see a ripple of pain approximately two to three inches long move from the top of Aaron's head down to his toes. Simultaneously, Aaron screamed, "Is the music off?" The educator quickly turned the tape over, started the music again, and within eight to ten minutes the ribbon of pain eased. Now much more comfortable, Aaron explained, "I told them not to turn the music off. I have no pain as long as the music is on." Over the next three weeks as his body prepared for death, Aaron's favorite Metamusic® for sleep was *Sleeping through the Rain*, but he turned to *Inner Journey* to "feel closer oneness with God" as he made his transition.

A similar example occurred with a five-year-old girl named Brittany who was dying. She craved *Sleeping in the Rain* and *Cloudscapes*, but *Inner Journey* was so deep she became scared. Within a week, both the parents and nurses recognized there was something very powerful about the music. Brittany did not need pain medicine when the music was on. Her expected timeline moved from three weeks to nine weeks. The last day she asked for *Inner Journey* to be played.

That same year several professional members who were also Reiki Masters[64] used Metamusic® tapes in Reiki sessions when they were invited into a hospital to help people in pain. One example is a five-year-old girl who had nearly drowned five weeks before their visit. As the Reiki Masters dialogued with the mother on how they might best assist, a nurse came in and aspirated the little girl's throat. Despite the fact that the child was in a "waking coma," her eyes looked terrified. The Reiki Masters asked the parents if they could play *Cloudscapes* to help the little girl relax. Within ten minutes of inserting the tape into a Fisher Price tape player and beginning the music, the father exclaimed, "Oh my God, look!" All present in the room turned to stare at the child in his lap. The muscles that had previously been rigid and contracted were now relaxed back to normal positions for the first time since the accident. A number of doctors and nurses came in to witness this "small miracle" and were amazed when shortly after the Metamusic® stopped, the girl's muscles tightened back up. *Cloudscapes* was used to relax the girl's muscles during the next year of physical therapy.

Several medical doctors began to use Metamusic® as part of their practices. Early examples included the playing of Metamusic® in the waiting room prior to surgeries and chemotherapy. Gari Carter (allergic to most anesthetics) made history and attracted many more people to the Professional Division when she used a specially-designed set of Hemi-Sync® tapes during surgery following a car accident. The surgery involved removing a rib to insert as a nose, refracturing and resetting the bones in the orbits around her eyes, and repairing her sinuses. Since she didn't totally trust the use of Hemi-Sync® she told the doctors and nurses to observe her, and if it didn't work to immediately give her codeine. Though the surgery lasted four and one-half hours, she never needed any pain medication during or afterwards and had minimal bruising and swelling. In the Recovery Room, every time she felt a twinge of pain begin she would put on her earphones and erase it. Healing was rapid in this relaxed state.[65] Gari Carter went on to write a book entitled *Healing Myself* detailing 22 other surgeries aided by the magic of Hemi-Sync®.

Moving Forward with Metamusic®

The continued successes attributed by the professional members across the country to the use of Metamusic® brought about development of three additional Metamusic® selections all enhanced by frequency following responses studied in the Monroe laboratories. These were: *Transformation* (by Mohammad Sadigh), *Prisms* (by Lenore Paxton and Phillip Siadi), and *Gaia* (by Richard Roberts). In support of physical wellness and spiritual development, *Transformation* included a journey through the tones representing the seven chakras. *Prisms* was designed to stimulate a whole-brain creative process for deeper relaxation. *Gaia* was a musical betrayal of Kokopelli, the Native American mythic hero who restores abundance by bringing forth the summer rains. The focus was on producing deeper, more profound meditation.

The first six of the Artist Series were a clear demonstration of the important synergistic effect when quality musical creations were combined with the power of Hemi-Sync® frequency following responses. There is an important creative merging that occurs when musical compositions are married with the intention of the underlying Hemi-Sync®. For example, specific keys represent specific feelings related to innate human responses.

In the ensuing years many other sound researchers expanded upon their own version of binaural beat aspects of Metamusic® including HeartMath® (Doc Lew Childre), the Center for Neuro Acoustic Research (Dr. Jeffrey Thompson) , BrainSync® (Kelly Howell), and others. As the feedback from these various forms of Metamusic® began to accumulate in other research organizations there was across-the-board a validation of the power behind the Hemi-Sync® Metamusic® approach.[66]

Chapter 7

Navigating the Interstate

By the Professional Division meeting of 1993 many of the members came with issues regarding the alarming rise of students with ADD and ADHD. In an early session, a discussion of research on ADD/ADHD children led by Robert Sornson, Ph.D., Executive Director of Special Education Services, Norville Public Schools, Michigan. He cites Dr. Daniel and others whose brain mapping indicated those with attention deficit had difficulty in maintaining the high levels of brain arousal associated with sustained alertness and focused attention. The research specifically showed an insufficiency of coordinated hemispheric brainwave patterns, especially with Beta brain waves in the left hemisphere for those with ADD. Because of all of the discussion Sornson went on to work with Hemi-Sync® using Beta harmonic sound patterns specifically designed to seek to increase the level of attention.[67]

The educators attending the Professional Division said that within a classroom of 30 students, one out of every three students would be identified as having ADD or ADHD. Further, it was noted that the number of boys affected outnumbered girls by three to one.

One attendee provided alarming statistics showing that by 10 years of age 25 percent of male students were on some sort of medication, primarily Ritalin. Research focused specifically on ADHD show that 65 percent of the children with ADHD displayed slow emotional development, and such problems as defiance, verbal hostility, temper tantrums and/or hyperactivity. Many of these children also had serious learning disabilities such as oral expression, listening skills, and reading or math comprehension.[68]

A discussion ensued that generated excitement amongst many of the gathered professionals. Did Metamusic® offer the potential for a non-drug solution? Would it be possible to use Beta Metamusic® to improve this growing problem in the educational system and the larger society? A subcommittee of the Professional Division was formed that conceived the idea of creating some super-learning music to combine Hemi-Sync® patterns with Beta. And thus began TMI's journey into supercharged learning.

Supercharging with Beta

In Chapter 2 we introduced the brain as an electrochemical system. In Chapter 6 we discussed the slower brainwave frequencies of Alpha, Theta and Delta. But it is Beta brainwaves (13-26 Hz) that have been identified as the most crucial to *focused attention* toward learning. Beta brainwaves move at the higher frequencies and have the most influence on the two hemispheres of the Cortex.

Brain mapping was extensively used by Dr. Daniel Amen as a method to determine the physical factors that could be connected to ADD and ADHD. In several hundred studies involving both children and adults, Amen discovered that the frontal lobes tended to *turn off rather than on* in individuals identified with ADD/ADHD. In his book, *Windows into the ADD Mind*, Amen writes:

When people with ADD try to concentrate, the frontal lobes of their brain (which control attention span, judgment, impulse control and motivation) decreased in activity. When normal control groups do concentration tasks, there is increased activity in this part of the brain. So, the harder these people try, the worse it gets for them.69

Although the research showed that Beta waves can create focused alertness and increased analytical capabilities, it was also discovered that adding Theta waves expanded learning. Theta waves provided the best imprint state and Beta waves the best problem-solving state. However, combining them posed a problem. Theta is the state of short duration *right before and right after* sleep, thus it was of short duration. This problem was solved by superimposing a Beta signal on the Theta signal, which produced a *relaxed alertness.*[70] This is consistent with findings from neurobiological research that efficient learning is related to a decrease in brain activation often accompanied by a shift of activation from the prefrontal regions to those regions relevant to the processing of particular tasks (the phenomenon known as the anterior-posterior shift).[71]

Supported by the subcommittee, Sornson agreed to do a double-blind research study with ADD/ADHD students using three different combinations (different harmonics) of Beta brain waves. Of the 20 students who completed the project, 16 of the 20 chose one particular combination of Beta brainwave frequencies as the most effective for their concentration.[72] Music appropriate for super-learning and peak performance states had then to be created that was complex enough to incorporate underlying Beta Hemi-Sync® tones. An enchanting composition was ultimately created by J.S. Epperson[73], a graduate of the USC School of Electronic Music, in collaboration with Barbara Bullard, an educator focusing on super-learning music. When testing the prototype from the research project, the lab tested frequencies in a piece titled *Concentration,* an early Mind Food® Hemi-Sync® product, was embedded on one side with the music and the pattern that was preferred by Sornson's ADD students was put on side B. This designer Metamusic® was titled *Remembrance* (with both parts A and B) and was launched by The Monroe Institute in 1994.

Remembrance

Bringing *Remembrance* into existence had proven a complex project. It was necessary to create a style of super-learning music that could be interwoven with the Beta Hemi-Sync® binaural beat, and this had not been previously tried. There were many early discoveries. For example, it turned out that the music was more effective in the key of "E" since music played in this key directly stimulates learning in the brain. It was also discovered that there were specific wave patterns that facilitated super-learning; for example, embedding a repeatable refrain. Further, it was found that a slower *chill-down piece* was required at the end of the piece in order to support learning integration in the pre-frontal cortex and lower parts of the brain.

As the use of Remembrance by Professional Division members expanded, Sornson reported that it was evident that this Beta Metamusic® was very effective in facilitating enhanced attention for students of high school and college age, as well as appropriate for use at home while doing homework. Further, he reported that students with ADD could benefit from listening to the tape on a portable cassette player with headphones in a classroom setting, and youngsters with neurologic delays, problems with cortical function, and developmental lags could also be helped by the Hemi-Sync® tapes. Similarly, Bullard reported a personal success where, after three months of using Remembrance, her 10-year-old son had out-grown his ADD and did not require the use of Ritalin. An additional observation reported by Sornson was that after listening to Hemi-Sync® over time youngsters seemed to develop a greater neurological capacity to integrate. They no longer seemed to need the external stimulus of Hemi-Sync® to access certain brainwave states.[74]

In the 1996 Professional Division Meeting, Debra Davis, a family therapist in Texas, presented a session titled, "Oh, the Stories I can Tell: Hemi-Sync® and Family Therapy"[75] which centered much around the surprising results of Remembrance. For example, a seven-year-old boy's mother brought him for counseling. He had been frequently wondering aloud what it would be like to die and was making comments about not being liked by other children or loved by his parents. His mother was remarried, with a new son, making this youngster the middle child. He was a somber, sober little guy and very intelligent, with a dry wit. After a psychiatric evaluation, he was given medication that relieved the obvious depression. However, he never acted spontaneous or happy in eight months of treatment.

As Davis described, "We'd play certain games each session. During one session I asked if he'd like to test some special music tapes and give me his opinion." She started with Remembrance. The response was almost immediate. Within two minutes the child asked if he could listen to Remembrance while playing the learning games. Davis agreed, saying she wanted him to try out some of the other tapes, too. However, the child didn't want to change from Remembrance. "I was puzzled," reflected Davis,

> … and waited to see what was up. He chose the first game, and we began to play. His energy level began to rise–subtly at first, then not so subtly. He looked at me, cracked jokes about the game, and began to tease me![76]

By the end of the session the child's energy and emotions were joyful, and he said, "I gotta have me one of these [tapes]!" Davis didn't mention changing tapes again since the results were so spectacular with Remembrance. It took his mother three weeks to get the tape, and two more weeks to get the tape player. However, Davis continued using Remembrance during her visits. One visit later the child was off all antidepressant medication, and follow-up visits to the psychiatrist were scheduled at three-month intervals rather than monthly.

As another example, a fourteen-year-old girl was referred for counseling by her caseworker at Child Protective Services. She and both her siblings had histories of severe abuse. In her foster home, she was having problems complying with rules. This child was always in motion of some kind during sessions and could not focus on any topic of conversation for more than a couple of minutes. Davis had only moderate success playing board games and card games as they talked. During the second session, Davis began some inner work—a process using relaxation and guided imagery. The girl listened to the original Concentration tape (without verbal guidance) and became still after about ten minutes, except for foot tapping and occasional peeks to check on Davis. The girl's foster parent later told Davis that the girl was upset at not being given a tape like that to keep with her. Evidently, she had experienced more relaxation than was apparent. During the third session Davis introduced *Remembrance* and several of the Metamusic® Artist tapes. The girl liked *Remembrance* best and easily stayed focused with it, so this piece was subsequently used for inner work. To date, Davis has used Metamusic® and the Metamusic® Artist table with over forty children. Without an exception, each child picked *Remembrance* as the number one favorite.[77]

Other reports received since 1994 indicate that Metamusic® such as *Remembrance* embedded with Beta Hemi-Sync® patterns may also help with learning disabilities beyond ADD and ADHD, specifically, dyslexia and slow-reading development, both of which have as an underlying cause a disparity of errors in timing between the two hemispheres. As one research reported,

> While reading, most good readers have left-hemisphere activity in the Beta range (around 13 Hz) and mid-range amplitude. Dyslexics, on the other hand, tend to have left hemisphere measurements in Alpha (roughly 10 Hz) and higher than average amplitudes, although some have unusually low amplitude … the cerebellum of dyslexics has not yet learned the coordination and timing involved in the internal balance of the body.[78]

It seemed from all of the reports that the synergistic combination of *designer music* with the Beta-harmonic Hemi-Sync® embedded frequencies did, in fact, help facilitate the necessary brain synchrony for focused attention. From the feedback pouring into The Monroe Institute and Professional Division members, *Remembrance* was being recognized as helping not just those with ADD/ADHD, but with the general population across ages for a wide variety of needs. Further, it seemed that *Remembrance* helped all learners study **smarter** rather than **harder**.

Mozart and the Hemi-Sync® Effect

By the middle of the 1990's, the *Mozart Effect* had become a meme, taking on a life of its own completely out of context of the findings. Perhaps this was because it was the first study relating music and spatial reasoning, suggesting that listening to music actually increased brain performance. There ensued high media coverage with the emphasis placed on the most sensational perceived findings. However, the details of the study—specifically, that these findings were limited to spatial reasoning not general intelligence, and that the effect was short-lived (10-15 minutes)—were not passed on as part of the meme.

In 1995, Rauscher, Shaw and Ky performed a follow-on study that was more extensive than the original study. This five-day study involved 79 college students who were pretested for their level of spatial/temporal reasoning prior to three listening experiences and then post-tested. While it was found that all students benefited (again, for a short period of time), the greatest benefits accrued to those students who had tested the lowest on spatial/temporal reasoning at the beginning of the experiment.[79]

By now, other groups were exploring the Mozart Effect. The results were similar to the earlier results, again for a short period of time.[80] However, a series of similar studies with slightly different approaches demonstrated no relevant differences between the group listening to Mozart and the control group.[81] Still another study began with the premise that the complex melodic variations in Mozart's sonata provided greater stimulation to the frontal cortex than simpler music. When this theory was tested it was discovered that the Mozart sonata activated the auditory as well as the frontal cortex in all of the subjects, thus suggesting a neurological basis for the Mozart Effect.[82] Other specific case results were emerging. For example, Johnson[83] reported improvement in spatial-temporal reasoning in an Alzheimer's patient; and Hughes[84] reported that a Mozart sonata reduced brain seizures.

As the exaggerated sensation of the initial finding began to sink into disillusionment, other researchers were building a deeper understanding of the effect. For example, it was determined that while listening to Mozart *before* testing might improve spatial/temporal reasoning, listening to Mozart *during* testing could cause neural competition through interference with the brain's neural firing patterns.[85] Studies expanded to include other musical pieces. The University of Texas Imaging Center in San Antonio discovered that "other subsets of music actually helped the experimental subjects do far better than did listening to Mozart."[86] Thus it was determined that the effect was not caused by the specific music of Mozart as much as the rhythms, tones or patterns of Mozart's music that enhanced learning. This is consistent with earlier work by researcher King[87] who suggested that there is no statistically significant difference between New Age music or Baroque music in the effectiveness of inducing Alpha states for learning (approximately 8-13 Hz), that is, they both enhance learning. However, Georgi Lozanov, a pioneer of accelerated learning, had said that classical and romantic music (circa 1750-1825 and 1820-1900, respectively) provided a better background for introducing new information,[88] and Clynes[89] had recognized a greater consistency in body pulse response to classical music than rock music, which means that the response to classical music was more predictable.[90]

Although there has been a considerable amount of controversy around the impact of the *Mozart Effect*, physics professor Dr. Gordon Shaw, researcher at UCI on the effects of music on the cortex and on learning, says, "It is not that Mozart will make you permanently smarter, but it may be a warm-up exercise for parts of the brain."

As Joshua Cooper Ramo reported in a *Newsweek* article on the impact of the Mozart Effect that, "Mozart's musical architecture evokes a sympathetic response from the brain, the way one vibrating piano string can set another humming."[92] For those who desire additional depth of information, an in-depth treatment of the human knowledge system, including the Mozart Effect, is included as Appendix B.

At each Professional Division gathering more and more success stories would come out about *Remembrance* and many of us began to wonder if it was the music, the Hemi-Sync® or, most likely, the synergy of the two. It was time to answer that question. The success of *Remembrance* paved the way for the creation of a second Metamusic® composition in 1996, which was destined to be a modification of Mozart's *Sonata for Two Pianos in D Major*, the same piece used in the initial study by Shaw and Rauscher which produced the controversial *Mozart Effect*. The Hemi-Sync® version, however, would include embedded combinations of Beta harmonics in order to encourage whole brain coherence. Bullard again collaborated with J. S. Epperson to design the Meta-Music® composition in which to embed Hemi-Sync®.[93]

The Launch of Einstein's Dream

The title *Einstein's Dream* was chosen for the new Beta Metamusic® offering because the Mozart Sonata being used was a favorite composition of Alfred Einstein, a great expert on Mozart. While built on the classical piece, *Einstein's Dream* had to be modified to incorporate the wave pattern of the repeatable refrain. This resulted in a level of irritation for those individuals used to hearing classical music and, in particular, Mozart. However, for the majority of listeners the modifications did not appear to be a problem. By 1997 many success stories were being shared about *Einstein's Dream*, and there were many observations recognizing that the combining of different music with the same frequencies created a totally different event.

Einstein's Dream proved very effective in learning detailed oriented subjects. For example, a 25-year-old man said,

Thank you for turning me on to Metamusic®. This is having a major impact on my life and education. I listen to *Einstein's Dream* every day, especially when I need to concentrate and energize. The other night I was studying so intensely that when the music clicked off, I jumped because it seemed like the loudest thing I'd ever heard … I was so focused in concentration. I turned the music on and continued. I was amazed that the difficult mathematical concepts came so easily to me while I was using it. The next day I got a perfect score on my math test.

As a second example, a 40-year-old man studying for a licensing exam stated:

With only one day to study for the State Insurance Licensing Exam, I thought it was hopeless. I'd never be able to remember a manual of 190 pages. I began studying at 9 AM and by 1 PM was losing my ability to concentrate. I then put *Einstein's Dream* into my continuous tape player and finished the book at 3 AM the next morning. I passed my test with 86 percent, thanks to *Einstein's Dream* which enabled me to maintain concentration for 18 hours.

A 37-year-old returning veteran from Iraq said he was very skeptical regarding the effectiveness of Metamusic®, but since he was getting a "D" in math he decided to try it out. Three weeks later he reported (along with an apology) that he was now up to a "B" and clearly there was something happening when he used Metamusic®. At the end of the semester he was studying in the library listening to *Einstein's Dream* on his headphones. If he got an "A" on his final exam, he would receive an "A" for the course. As he focused on his math studies, he physically felt the sensation of his heart expanding and simultaneously his wife's face came into his consciousness. He realized he'd been very abrupt with her because of his extensive study time, and felt he needed to go home and tell her he loved her. The teacher responded to his story, "That must be the Beta endorphins." Then the student continued,

Yes, but my heart kept expanding and my kid's faces came into my mind, and I realized I needed to spend more time playing with them. My heart kept expanding, I looked at everybody in the library, and I realized I loved them too! So I took the headphones off and took a break. That night I went home and told my family how much I loved them. And the next day I got an "A" in my math class.

Learning Along the Path

A number of reoccurring patterns were emerging as the use of and feedback from Beta Metamusic® increased. It was clear that Beta Hemi-Sync® combined with super-learning formats was quite effective. It also became clear that the rhythms and the instrumentation of the music created a unique Metamusic® piece each time in terms of learning support. Further, there seemed to be **a transaction that occurred with each individual**. An individual had to *enjoy* the musical format or there was a reduction of the effectiveness of Hemi-Sync® in their learning.

Another lesson learned was that the impact of *Einstein's Dream* versus *Remembrance* was decidedly different. No doubt this was partly due to the intense piano composition of *Einstein's Dream* versus the more New Age, softer effect of *Remembrance*. Some people had a great preference for the tones of *Remembrance*, whereas others had a preference for the piano-driven *Einstein's Dream*. In particular, males who were ADHD needed the faster music for focus.

When professional members used *Einstein's Dream* with their clients, they discovered that it served an interesting niche, that is, it seemed extremely helpful for students with their hardest subjects, in particular, with math, physics and science. The more intense rhythms appeared to "wake up" the brain, affecting an individual's neurochemistry. Similarly, Albert Einstein wrote that music—especially Mozart's music—made him acutely aware of the underlying mathematical structure. This awareness, in turn, focused his concentration.

Given that Beta Metamusic® was used as a sonic background (see Chapter 5), *Remembrance* seemed to work better for focus on and memory of the pattern recognition involved in global thinking. For example, in contrast with the successful use of *Einstein's Dream* supporting students in the areas of math, physics and science, *Remembrance* worked well in supporting students working in the areas of History, Psychology, Geography and English. Over the years Bullard has discovered that most students incorporating Metamusic®, particularly *Einstein's Dream* and *Illumination*, can move quickly from "D's" and "F's" to "A's" and "B's". Music supercharges the learning effect and increases retention and recall.

There seemed to be for many a correlation between using the Beta Metamusic® and a lifting of mood or depression, suggesting that there may be a chemical release of Beta endorphins triggered by the electrical Beta brainwaves flowing through the Cortex. These have been known to lead to a joy of learning.

One psychiatrist used *Remembrance* and *Einstein's Dream* for students with depressive syndrome, especially those with memory difficulties and whose ability to concentrate was diminished due to depression. All of these students had problems with concentration, attention-to-task deficit, lack of short-term memory, and felt unable to perform mental tasks as well as they had previously. The patients liked the effectiveness of the tapes, and reported improvement in their ability to concentrate during test preparation and other cognitive tasks, better short-term memory, greater interest in their studies, and an ability to sustain attention for longer periods than was previously possible.

As a final example, a 57-year-old man from Texas who had heard about Metamusic® decided to purchase *Remembrance*. As he listened, twenty minutes into the first half he realized he was still blaming himself for a mistake he had made seven years previously. He felt that the music began to cleanse him of the impact of his feelings of guilt, and as the music began to play the second time he found himself forgiving himself for the mistake, and through cleansing tears let go of a seven-year depression. He is convinced that *Remembrance* allowed this shift.

Expanding Choices

There was a clamoring for more choices from professional members working with a variety of age groups and different needs; from learners with diversity of musical preferences; and from students using it in a super-learning sense needing a wider selection of music to match with different subjects. In 2002 J. S. Epperson released a follow-up Beta Metamusic® called *Indigo for Quantum Focus* and Scott Bucklin, a musician from Texas, released *Seasons at Robert's Mountain*, which incorporated extracts from Vivaldi's *Four Seasons*. Since much of the seminal research of super-learning focused on Baroque adagio selections, *Four Seasons* seemed like an excellent match for a Beta super-learning piece. Adding another selection, Joshua Leeds, author of *The Power of Sound*, collaborated with The Monroe Institute to release *Baroque Garden*. Feedback from these three offerings further documented the effectiveness of Beta Metamusic® in aiding learning.[94]

By the early part of the century a digital divide was prevalent. Younger generations demanded greater choices in musical selections, with a greater variety of musical instrumentation and faster music. Indeed, perhaps this was one indicator that brains were speeding up. By 2004 there were regular releases of Beta Metamusic® and a greater variety of choices. These proved extremely valuable for the Net Generation, who seemed to favor the newer musical selections, many of which are synthesizer music often performed by trance musicians.

For a good indication of your personal preferences, listen to the short melodic excerpts of Metamusic® included on the www.Hemi-Sync.com and www.higher-music.com websites. The faster selections are: *Illumination* (J. S. Epperson), *Breakthrough* (Michael Maricle), and *Elation* (Michael Maricle).

The three classical pieces are *Lightfall* (Lenore Paxton and Phillip Siadi), *Guitara Classica* (Felix Rodriguez) and *Golden Mind* (J. S. Epperson). *Lightfall* is comprised of three Bach pieces including *Thus Spach Zarathrustra* with the theme song from Space Odyssey 2001, which many teachers are finding works very well in the classroom setting. *Golden Mind* is an adaptation of Bach's Goldberg variations that were created for King Ludwig to entertain him during his bouts of insomnia when everyone else was asleep. In addition to the Beta embedded in *Golden Mind*, there are some experimental binaural beats which help facilitate new creative thought. Of all the Beta Metamusic®, *Guitara Classica* is the single offering that is string instrumentation, not a synthesizer. The musician is a Flamenco guitarist who was trained by the world-renown Segovia.

Different combinations of these Beta Metamusic® are used by many learners. One mature college student reported that she used *Illumination* for writing essays and collecting research data to efficiently organize it as clearly and concisely as possible; *Breakthrough* for complex chemical processes and complicated anatomical diagrams (which raised her grade from an "F" to a "B"); and *Remembrance* to help with Pharmacology and remembering drug contra-indications and differences between certain drug classifications. As she wrote in an essay entitled "The Wonders of Hemi-Sync® in a Crazy World":

It was the mechanics of the music, the way it draws you in, and being at first, unaware, starts to sharpen your focus, like a jeweler cutting a priceless diamond, which will change the processes in your brain to create value there, substance and power. We all need an edge in this fast-paced competitive world, but most of the time the way comes at our own expense. It comes at the risk of losing our health, our relationships, or our lives at the outmost extreme. This is why this avenue of achieving and competing where it is healthy and rewarding without the detriment is *beyond words*.

Many professional members have incorporated Beta and Alpha music in the classroom. A shining example is the work of Carmen Mototo who uses Metamusic® and Hemi-Sync® combined with the principles of Brain Gym®. The effectiveness of her research results has led to the creation of several learning centers in Puerto Rico. This work is so powerful that we invite you to read about it in Appendix C.

Chapter 8

Voices Along the Highways

By Junior High School and onward into High School and College, students have hopefully begun to realize the vital role they play in learning. Following adolescence, **learning is not something that happens to us—it's something we *choose* to do.**

Now that we know some of the neuroscience behind Metamusic® and Hemi-Sync®, let us gain inspiration as we hear voices of student learners, teachers and others and how they have discovered greater success on the pathways of learning. The examples below were primarily collected during the last decade from young College students.

Did Metamusic® help these learners study **smarter, not harder**?

When VK listens to *Remembrance*, it makes her feel energetic and eager to learn. "Like I craved knowledge as I used it for studying. While she used to feel bored and drained by studying. "So, I would push myself and that gave me a lot of pressure and anxiety … This also made me feel depressed and stupid when I wasn't able to remember or know the subject." After listening to *Remembrance* everything turned around for her, and her grades rapidly improved. WPW listens to *Remembrance* or *Einstein's Dream* when he is studying. He recalls, "I hope this doesn't sound strange, but once I felt as if my brain had physically connected when I was listening to these. I also felt that my brain grew larger."

MN says studying with Metamusic® is very helpful. When he first heard about it, he just wanted to try it out and see how it worked, so he bought *Illumination*. "I am really impressed with how much it helps me. When I listen to the music, my brain is totally awake and I can learn more easily." He actually feels the music inside his brain. In his words, "I can feel the music going through the front of my brain, to the middle and to the back, waking up every nerve in my brain."

AR has been familiar with the Hemi-Sync® music for almost two years and has been listening to the different CDs … "I committed to listening for a period of six weeks in a row, every day and night. I would like to admit that I definitely feel that listening to the CD's has helped me in so many different ways in all areas of my life."

Increased Focus and Concentration

DN feels that *Remembrance* is remarkable. "It is compiled with some of the most unique and beautiful music I ever heard." When she listens to it while studying or writing it keeps her calm, collected and concentrating with ease, sharpening her focusing skills. "Even when a deadline is fast approaching, I don't panic or feel like I'm being pressured or rushed. MN says *Remembrance* is really good for concentration. "Usually, when I study, my mind is easily distracted by everything around me." But when he listens to Hemi-Sync® while studying, he can concentrate and not get distracted by his surroundings. He adds, "It also helps me to accomplish things faster."

B says that *Breakthrough* not only sounds good, but allows him to concentrate on whatever task he is performing. "I am listening to it as I am writing this essay, and I have no doubt that without this CD I would not be able to write this paper." B reflected that he had not been able to write more than four pages ever in his life because he can't get himself to sit down and concentrate long enough, which discourages him. But, with *Breakthrough* playing behind him, "the words just seem to flow to my hands as I type along, which is why I love this CD so much."

BA also used *Elation* regularly. In fact, this is his personal favorite. He uses this CD when he needs help focusing on a homework assignment. "The upbeat electro music really gets my mind flowing, and in a short time I become very focused on the task at hand." He also musically enjoys the compilation of tracks on *Elation*, which he compares to *Revelations*. He then adds, "The only thing I did not like about this CD is that it's not long enough!!"

* * * * *

*Learners can utilize the knowledge gained from the Neuroscientific research
to tap into and awaken their own "genius within."*
-Barbara Bullard

* * * * *

MB uses *Lightfall* anytime he needs to focus on something, but mostly when he is writing papers or doing other schoolwork. "When I listen to *Lightfall*, it seems as though my brain syncs and I am able to think clearly." Even when playing video games he notices that he actually plays better and smarter!

HP used *Einstein's Dream* and *Seasons at Roberts Mountain* as study aides. During an internship at the Regional Medical Center, a resident physician told HP that the worst part of getting an undergraduate degree was trying to get through all of the classes that didn't interest you but were needed for a degree, not a career. HP recalls, "I have always had trouble in those classes. I have difficulty focusing on things I find boring or tedious." While he still finds those assignments boring, he now can keep his attention on them long enough to finish in a reasonable time period. "I find myself able to focus better on every subject while listening to the CD and I'm noticed my attention span without he CD has improved." He quickly adds that he has never been diagnosed with ADD or any attention disorder, nor does he think he has a disorder, but whatever it is that's causing his lack of focus, his condition has improved significantly with Metamusic®.

Increased Retention and Recall

Chapter 6 introduced Metamusic® as an aid to learning and memory. Along the way many students have commented on the enhanced retention. For example, DP notices that when she uses *Remembrance* she is able to retain the information a lot faster and easier than she had been doing. She relates one experience that was a very imaginative and visual one.

I kind of felt like the information I was reading was like little sparkly particles in the air that bonded to the sound waves of the music. As the sound waves went into my ears and through my brain, the sparkles of information stayed in my brain, and the sound waves proceeded to go out of the other ear.

It was really weird because in my mind I pictured all of the information I had acquired as little boxes when the professor mentioned the topic I had been studying with Hemi-Sync®. I felt like they had opened one of the boxes, and that all the information I had learned was floating in my brain like pieces of a puzzle, floating around randomly. Every topic that he mentioned was a piece of the puzzle, and as he kept talking, I knew exactly which piece of the puzzle he was referring to, and I just kept picking out pieces of the puzzle and putting them together, and at the end of the lecture, I had the whole concept down in a nice big puzzle picture.

EA comments on the super-enriched whole-brain state of Metamusic®. "When needing to read some highly technical papers, I experimented with and without *Remembrance*. The difference really impressed me. When listening to the CD I was much more able to attend to the content, stay focused, and didn't have to reread sentences for comprehension, etc. as I listened to *Remembrance* more and more, I noticed that I started to hear it less. I actually didn't even notice that it was playing. This is when the greater benefits started showing. I was studying for a major test which required lots of formulas and memorization. With Metamusic® the concepts came easily to me. I got a perfect score on the test."

MN notes that "When I took a test the other day, I could hear the music in my brain all of a sudden. This allowed me to quickly recall what I studied."

Synergy between Metamusic® and the Study Environment

Chapter 5 introduced the idea of setting up a rich learning environment to support Super Learning. As you read the responses below, it is clear that these community college students have begun to understand and apply these concepts. For example, VR has created a peaceful setting with incense burning the room in an isolated place meant to serve as a study area alone. "With everything put together, I feel I am a more productive person and that if I really invest in the studying environment, I can see and feel the result in myself."

RA has tried all the super learning techniques described in Chapter 5. He initially experimented with these techniques while studying for his Business Law class. Each time he would read the chapters or study for a test, he would listen to Metamusic®. He made sure that for each subject he studied, he was studying in the same place. "I chose the desk in my room and made sure it was always quiet in the room." He always tried to study before going to sleep or when he would wake up. He noticed that when he did this his mind would soak in the information he was reading much better than if he were reading in the middle of the day when there were other things to worry about.

RA also practiced bilateral breathing. "This helped me to be calm and feel relaxed as I was studying." He also used positive affirmations before, during and after studying. "This helped me to believe in myself. Once you believe in yourself, you can do a lot more. I kept telling myself that I loved Business Law and that I knew I was the smartest one in the class; I knew I could get an 'A' in my next test." And every 30-40 minutes (without any interruptions) he would take a quick break. "This really helped me to re-energize my brain." When it came time for RA to take the test for his Business Law class, he felt relaxed and confident going in and after he finished the test he knew he had done very well. He made the 'A'. As he sums up, "These techniques are very useful and I anticipate using them in future classes."

N has created his personal learning environment. He sits in his living room surrounded by candles with affirmations in front of him. As he listens to *Lightfall* he feels bathed in positivity from all angles. "Since making my environment comfortable for me to study in, I have made my studies more successful." He controls the setting so that he can focus, and feel the content growing my knowledge. "I keep thinking of the 'fun' and the pleasure that all of this new knowledge has brought me. I enjoy it all with a kind of geekish glee!"

Individual Student Approaches for Specific Subjects

By this time students have discovered that there are certain subjects that are harder or more difficult for them than others, and this can continue into the college experience and throughout life. Metamusic® and Hemi-Sync® can play a vital role in helping students of all ages absorb topics in and out of the classroom that don't fit as easily into an individual's specific brain. Below are a series of direct quotes from community college students that communicate their Metamusic® choices for studying various subjects.

Mathematics

A number of the quotes below refer to *Buy the Numbers*. This is a Human Plus® CD focused on sharpening skills for working with numbers in everyday applications and improving an individual's aptitude for defining and understanding numerical concepts.

CS first used *Buy the Numbers* because he was not doing well in his math class. "I had a C-, but I wanted an A or a B. By the time I got this CD, the only hope I had of raising my grade was doing well on the final. I had to get an A on it in order to earn a B in the class. I studied very hard while listening to the CD. I found that it helped me to not get distracted and to want to learn and understand the material. Well, test day came and I got an A on the final. I was so happy and excited."

RC used *Einstein's Dream* with his math homework. "I could tell a difference right away. I was able to remember things that I learned in class that I usually forget by the time I get to my homework. I was amazed that on my next math test, I got an A. This was the first time that I EVER got an A on a math test."

BM's first introduction to Metamusic® was *Einstein's Dream*. He used it to assist him in studying for his math class. "During the semester I was having difficulty sitting down and doing my homework. That would then result in me doing it quickly before the test and not really absorbing and retaining the information. After I bought this CD, I would use my hour and a half break on campus to find a nice quiet place where I could sit down to study with my walkman. Instead of it being a hassle, it soon became a much more pleasant experience and I was really absorbing the information. I went from a C average to getting an A on the final and a B in the class."

VV says "*Einstein's Dream* was my next purchase and I was about to embark on the most mentally taxing task I have ever encountered … math homework! I am one that prefers colors and shapes to numbers and graphs so this was going to be the ultimate test to see if Hemi-Sync® was as amazing as everyone claimed. I popped in the CD and started my tedious mission. I was pleasantly surprised that the music was uplifting and the distraction level was little to none. I was quite astonished that I not only finished my math homework but I checked the answers in the back of the book and I was correct on 98 percent of the problems. This proved that not only could I sit there and finish two sections, but that I actually understood it … I am making sure that *Einstein's Dream* is nearby my study place."

EK has been using *Golden Mind* for math. "I was a little sceptical at first, I really wasn't sure how a CD would improve my math skills. Soon after listening I started to concentrate on what I was doing. It's not that the music was making me more intelligent and I was suddenly getting it, but I understood it better because I was concentrated on the work itself. I used it throughout the week to study for my math test and would only turn it on for my math and nothing else. When it came time for the test I went to the math center but I was a little scared because I was not going to be able to have headphones on during the test. When I sat down, I took a few deep breaths and started thinking about the music. It seemed like I had remembered so much. I soon gained more confidence and concentrated on the test. I ended up passing with 97 percent on the test, one of the best scores I have ever received in math."

JH says "One of my classes this semester is a math class, College algebra. I have been pretty nervous all semester taking it because this is the only class holding me back from transferring. After listening to *Remembrance* for a couple of weeks, I started to notice a change in my studying habits of my math class; my math class is an online class which emails many homework sections and chapter quizzes. I started to notice that when it came time to take my quizzes I could recap information better than before. I began to remember information for my quizzes off the top of my head instead of having to look back in my notes and try to relearn them again."

Statistics

CEG was a working adult taking classes at night. He was struggling through his Statistics class, and needed a "B" on the final example just to pass the class. A friend gave him *Elation* to listen to while he studied for the final. "The night before the test, I played the tape and studied the class fundamentals. I went to bed early, not feeling much more confident about my upcoming exam. The next day, while taking the exam, I tried to relax and "hear the music" in my head. I felt okay about my performance but not great. When I received my grade, however, I was amazed. I had passed the class. I called the school's voice response system over and over to hear my grade, thinking that perhaps I had heard wrong. But no—it was true, and I believe that I have Hemi-Sync® to thank."

Science

When AR read school material, especially for his science classes, he found it to be very challenging and sometimes even seem somewhat complicated. "I found that when I play one of the Metamusic® CDs, even without using headphones, I can say that within a few minutes I feel more focused and much more relaxed. I feel that after the struggle of actually sitting down and trying to read, I can get in the 'trance' of learning and receiving information as soon as I begin to listen to these wonderful sounds. I am not feeling sleeping and I am able to focus without reeling distracted. When I listen as I read, I find that my thoughts are not wandering around. My mind is not looking for something else to be occupied with."

BCBN says of his use of *Lightfall,* "This CD really amazed me. I was able to study less but get better grades. For example, in my molecular biology class, I got a 90 percent on my first exam, 95 percent on my second one, and a 96 percent on the third. I did not study very much for these, but when I did study I would listen to this CD. I have to say that not only did my academic performance improve, but my performance at work improved as well."

DA has seen some amazing changes. "This semester I finally mustered up the courage to take Chemistry, the last class I needed … Science has always been an uphill battle for me … All the tests from the semester were merely quizzes, from hell of course. The exam the following morning would either make or break my grade in the class up to that point. But we had just gone over the Hemi-Sync® tapes in class that day and [a friend] thought it would be a good idea to give *Einstein's Dream* a try. She thought it would help me focus a little longer and concentrate a little better. So we slipped the CD in, pressed play, and I prayed that *Einstein's Dream* would do its magic … I am not a big fan of classical music, but after some time, I just forgot that the music was even on. But it did its magic anyways, because without me even noticing it, my focus and concentration had increased significantly. I never looked at the clock and panicked that it was getting too late, never got sidetracked with my cat, didn't constantly get up and move around, and, perhaps the most important thing, didn't miss any of these things, didn't even think of them. It wasn't as though I was trying to force the CD to work, it just did. Not only did it help with the concentration while studying, it also helped with my memory and concentration during the exam."

CT found, "With Metamusic®, particularly *Breakthrough,* I have been able to read more information faster and understand it much better and relate it to the diagrams I the book. My lab team and I have been testing Hemi-Sync® on each other. It has been challenging though because of all the distractions we have in our lab. But the students have claimed and our test scores have shown that Metamusic® does help with memory. *Breakthrough* has helped me a lot by helping me to relax and therefore concentrate better, hence absorbing much more information."

Social Sciences and History

DK purchased *Einstein's Dream* and *Buy the Numbers* because he was fascinated by the brain and what music can do. He started listening to *Buy the Numbers* each night. While he didn't think anything was actually working, he would sleep very soundly and wake up rejuvenated. Then things started to change. "One day I started having a study group with some friends for my Political Science class. In this class, we had to know dates of certain cases and events in history. One of my peers was asking a date of a particular case and how many people it affected. To my surprise, I said the answer without any hesitation. All of the students in my study group were shocked, including me."

RC says, "*Remembrance* was the first CD that I tried. At first, it was not what I expected. I thought the sounds would be more natural. But I gave the CD a chance. I put it in while I was readying my political science book. I hate political science, and haven't been able to comprehend more than two pages at a time out of that book. To my surprise, by the end of the whole CD, I had read an entire chapter. Not only did I read the whole chapter, but I retained a lot of the information."

AS listened to *Illumination* a lot of the times when he was reading for his sociology class. "I didn't really notice a difference at first. But as time progressed I started noticing a difference when I would have conversations with my sister about the things I was learning. I would talk to her and remember everything that I learned and it got to the point where I started quoting the book."

Reading and Writing with Ease

OB originally purchased *Remembrance* and *Elation last* semester to use while writing a report for a Business Communications class. As he relates, "The results of listening to Metamusic® while writing my report were astounding. I was amazed at how much focus and concentration I now possessed. It was like I could tune the whole world out; the only thing I was aware of was the music in my head and the report in front of me. Moreover, Ideas would come to me much more quickly and easily than before. I was literally watching a paper write itself before my eyes. I felt as though I was putting no effort into it at all. Most of all, my endurance had increased tenfold. I could research books for my report for hours on end and I would continue retaining the critical information I needed to write an informative and concise paper."

DN finds that she writes more easily than ever before."I can feel my creative juices flowing when I listen to *Remembrance*. I can feel my mind clear and my heart open up to endless possibilities." She adds, "I know for sure how effective it is when I am writing or doing anything artsy … [and] the most enchanting part is that if my body is kind of tired, I can feel myself fill with warm energy. I can feel myself coming alive again."

JR found this same coming alive feeling when he states, "When I used *Remembrance* my homework flowed more easily, and it felt very natural and not at all straining on my mind. Usually when I am typing a paper I run into many writer blocks, but with this Metamusic® I was able to recall new ideas and comments easily, and I found myself much more attentive to my writing. This is pretty new to me;

I usually dread writing papers and procrastinate to the max. The practice of using Metamusic® will be with me throughout college now that I am aware of the effects of it and how helpful it is."

Enhanced Creativity

The impact of Metamusic® transcends subject matter to more global areas of thinking and felling such as enhancing creativity.

JG says, "*Remembrance* gives me a tug back to the subject at hand ... when reading, I listen with headphones and find my concentration much deeper. For doing creative work, I sit between speakers, and the CD produces a feeling of balance, sustained energy, and the ability to zero in on tasks. I experience heightened awareness, absence of distractions, greater absorption and a depth of focus. Thank you for the sonic environment for creativity!"

AA noticed when listening to *Radiance* that when the music took a strange turn or made a juristic musical change—like the addition of an instrument for the first time—he would look at a problem or the situation at hand in a completely different manner than before. "The music subconsciously would open my mind to new ways of looking at or solving a problem. This was interesting to me how certain tunes and frequencies can trigger a different feeling or part of the brain."

BA chose CDs for creativity and focus. He found the Metamusic® used for creativity was very smooth and natural, while the music for increased concentration was upbeat and flowing. He discovered that *Revelations* "is great when you need bursts of creativity energy such as for writing papers and drawing." He added this CD to his routine.

SE says that while listening to *Remembrance*, "My brain seemed to be open to anything, for everything was clear. I was doing homework from one of my classes and felt more creative as the music played in the background."

VK turns on *Radiance* when she is drawing. While she used to hesitate on certain things she was drawing, when the CD is playing things are different. "I feel like I can draw anything and my hand just feels like it is moving on its own. Everything flows and there are major changes in my art work as well." Her artwork and ideas now flow more freely.

AM purchased *Illumination* because he was a performer and competitor for a Forensics team, which requires him to have the energy, creativity and confidence to perform at any given moment. As he describes, "After performing the same four pieces over and over again for months, the creative spontaneity and passion gets a bit difficult to tap into." He now listens to *Illumination* a couple of days before the tournament. "It is a great way for me to calm down, center myself and focus my energy before a big tournament." Feeling relaxed and confident, there is space for his creativity to emerge.

Resonating with Remembrance

It's clear that when motivated students and adults incorporate Metamusic® and Hemi-Sync®. They can create magical learning outcomes. But what about the challenged learner? One story from New York's alternative school system gives us insights. Peter Spiro, a playwright and poet,

Last year started like any other year. My classroom is a basement room in a building in a housing project. And there are the students: restless, disturbed, fatigued, undernourished, fearful, and on edge. So, I bought a boom box with detachable speakers, spread the speakers out along the back of the room, and began one day by playing Hemi-Sync®, the tape of *Remembrance*. I expected nothing. One particular kid, who normally survives each day by emulating the behavior of a monkey on a pogo stick, took a seat up front and quietly completed each assignment efficiently and timely. Most of the class thought he was absent! Still, I doubted whether the tape alone had helped him achieve this state of contentment.

But the same thing happened the next day, and every day thereafter as long as *Remembrance* was spinning in the boom box. I finally had to accept that the tape was actually performing as advertised. Even the kid knew this: he'd pass me with a wink and say, "Hey Pete you're trying to calm me down with that brain music, right?" And so, I ordered a variety of Metamusic® tapes and played them all day long. The kids thought the music was weird and joked a lot about it. They couldn't understand why there were no vocal accompaniments, and they were pretty sure it was either Indian or Arabic in origin. They'd roll their eyes and shake their heads, but if I forgot to lay a tape they'd pipe with, "Hey Pete, what happened to the brain music?"

They liked it even if they didn't readily admit it. I started handing out tapes to play in their portable tape players. I'd catch a few secretly listening to something else with lots of bass and volume. But the majority just sat there listening to Metamusic®, quietly performing various tasks. It became a ritual. A kid would come up to me and ask for a "brain tape," then return to his seat and do the assignment. The first time I played *Concentration* for the group you'd swear—if you didn't know where you were—that the class was a prep school for serious students totally focused on some scholarly pursuit. I just sat and observed. when the tape ended, they all began to move and talk and drop pencils—which is their usual approach to scholarship.

I have looked out on the room as a Metamusic® tape played and seen a kid's face so open, so pure and innocent, so peaceful he could have passed for a cherub. And I like to think the "brain tapes" helped get him there, if only for a short time.

Moving into Harmony

When using Metamusic® for study or attaining peak performance, it is best to treat it as a sonic background. If it is used consistently while studying, you need only to allow your favorite portions of the refrain to flow through your awareness and the information you studied will be more readily accessed. The music is especially effective when used in tandem with some other Hemi-Sync® exercises (such as using *Buy the Numbers* with *Einstein's Dream* for math). Other students found *Attention, Think Fast* and *Retain-Recall-Release* especially helpful.

We have heard from so many Voices Along the Highways; we have only shared a few in this chapter. Although many parents and teachers have found these beta-harmonic compositions to be highly effective tools for learning, they should not be regarded as "magic bullets." Rather they should be treated as helpful aids to lead the brain gently into an alert and attentive state of consciousness.

A sixty-year-old engineer who had suffered for many years with a medical diagnosis of "cognitive brain collapse" reported quite poetically after using *Remembrance* for two months:

Remembrance is like breathing clean air; it's even better than a box of chocolates! It offers a gentle, three-dimensional support. It calms the scattering, allows the centering, like a pleasant non-noticeable incense. I find myself now able to lead the project rather than push the project ... With *Remembrance* I don't have to conquer tasks but can guide them simply and effectively. **Remembrance is the difference between harmony and heartburn; as a helper, it allows me to allow.**

Chapter 9

Crossing the Rainbow Bridge

While Beta brainwaves are crucial to the waking state (the learning state where you anchor in new learning) the Alpha, Theta, and Delta brainwave states are equally crucial to balance the many other levels of the triune brain. Long before recognition of the power of Beta embedded in Metamusic®, The Monroe Institute was using combinations of Alpha, Theta and Delta to achieve relaxation, healing, meditation and sleep.

For optimum health, Steven Halpern, Ph.D., a well-known creator of healing music, suggests listening to music with an Alpha/Theta brainwave rhythm for a minimum of 30 minutes per day. Halpern bases this statement, in part, on an understanding of the correlation between vibrations in the earth's electromagnetic field and those of the human body. The earth vibrates at an inaudible frequency of approximately eight cycles per second. When the human body is deeply relaxed, it too vibrates at approximately eight cycles per second. This sympathetic resonance is known as Schumann's Resonance, and it implies that being in *harmony* with oneself and the Universe may be more than a mere concept.[95]

This idea of harmony is a core issue behind the creation of Metamusic®. The composer cannot "show off" but must "blend in" to incorporate each melody with care so that it leads and guides specific desired states of consciousness. When he was TMI Chief Recording Engineer, Mark Certo, said,

> The ability to incorporate symphony orchestras and create sounds which are not easily definable—yet are aesthetically pleasing—gives an unprecedented compositional freedom to our composers. The results are phenomenal. Metamusic® is expressive, soulful, and spans the generation gap. The freedom of expression is not only the composers, but is a shared experience between composer and listener.[96]

The stresses of modern man tend to keep many of us caught in a disorganized Beta state, which produces an accumulation of stress. For physical wellness it's important for each individual to return to a more balanced state. Many people choose to do this in their sleep state.

We read daily articles that say our nation is sleepy. According to the National Institutes of Health more than 30-50 million people in the United States suffer from various forms of insomnia or sleep disorders. This becomes alarming since insomnia of all kinds has been related to an increased risk of medical problems, including high blood pressure and depression, accidents, and lower productivity at work. Michael Twery, Director of the National Center on Sleep Disorders Research, a Division of the NIH, says, "Mounting evidence indicates that sleep may be as important as diet and physical activity for a healthy life style."[97] He goes on to say that getting a good night's sleep is necessary for both cardiovascular and metabolic health, and that insufficient sleep directly affects the way individuals see the world as well as their mood, performance, vigilance, awareness, and the ability to perceive the environment and respond to challenges.[98]

When people are this sleep deprived, their concentration drops and they suffer memory lapses. The brain can fall into *rigid thought patterns*, which makes problem solving and decision-making difficult, and obviously can have a big impact on personal and professional performance. But even more crucial, about 85 percent of individuals suffering from sleep disorders say that other health problems also arise because of these. One of the biggest losses to modern business is the sleep-deprived night-shift worker. It amounts to roughly $17 Billion per year. Further, roughly 40 percent of teenagers report sleep deficiencies. This becomes a definite problem in our schools since poor sleepers report being less alert and significantly more tired, moody, irritable and depressed.

Metamusic® for Supersleep

Because of the growing need for sleep aids, The Monroe Institute began in the 1970's to carefully design sleep induction systems which use specific sound patterns to regulate the sleep cycle. Robert Monroe, Ph.D., recognized that the easiest way to affect any culture is to respond to a widespread need. As he explained,

> Such a need can be found in the daily process that we identify as sleep. It consumes one-third of human existence, an area about which little is known, little or no conscious control is exercised, and of which little use is made other than the obvious.[99]

The Hemi-Sync® system works because of its unique design which includes sleep-state-specific binaural sound waves. Each stage of sleep is induced at the appropriate time in the sleep cycle with uniquely human wave patterns. As Skip Atwater explained when he was the Director of Research for The Monroe Institute:

Rather than simply selecting Beta, Alpha, Theta, or Delta sine-wave binaural beats to stimulate the various sleep stages, human sleep-wave patterns were developed with the aid of computerized EEG recording equipment. Brain-wave recordings from a number of sleeping subjects were categorized according to sleep stages. Then, characteristic wave forms for each stage of sleep were combined mathematically to produce a unique waveform for each sleep stage. These human-sleep-stage wave forms were then converted into sleep-stage-specific Hemi-Sync® binaural beats.

Consistent use of these Hemi-Sync® sound patterns at night encourages the formation of natural sleep cycles. The Metamusic® masks background noise and shifts attention away from disrupting sleep-incompatible activities. Sleep-stage-specific binaural beat sound waves induce Alpha/Theta/Delta brainwave patterns, and then changes in consciousness create natural REM sleep.

J. Alan Hobson, M.D., Professor of Psychiatry at Harvard Medical School, says that it is crucial to have deep REM (Rapid Eye Movement) sleep stages. He calls these sleep cycles *supersleep* because it is during the REM sleep cycles that the immune-activating healing response occurs.[100] Unfortunately, Dr. Hopson continues, too many people because of the stress of the day are going into non-REM (NREM) sleep, which is non-rejuvenating. During REM sleep the brain is known to be extremely active consolidating the memory of the day in the dream state. This is also where the stresses of the day are discharged. Thus, the more NREM sleep (and less REM sleep) the more tired you are when you awake.[101]

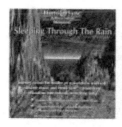   

The original form of *Supersleep* was pink noise, or surf sounds masking the sleep-induction tones of Hemi-Sync®. With the introduction of the Artist Series Metamusic®, *Sleeping Through the Rain, Midsummer Night, Cloudscapes* and *Transformation* became more enjoyable alternatives to pink noise or surf sounds. The Artist Series over the past decades have become widely popular such that new releases come out annually, often making it difficult to discern the best treatment for a specific desired outcome. The following tables include some of the author's preferred collections of Metamusic® and Hemi-Sync® for the variety of needs fulfilled by Alpha, Beta and Delta modalities.

Table 9-1 provides selected Metamusic® favorites that induce/support the REM sleep state. Consistent with the sleep-stage-specific approach taken by The Monroe Institute, all of these selections combine elements of Alpha/Theta/Delta brainwave patterns.

TABLE 9-1: Selected Metamusic® for Sleep

TITLE	DESCRIPTION	OBSERVATIONS
Angel Paradise	Irish harp.	Angelic harp providing supportive comfort level.
Cloudscapes	Synthesizer.	Like floating on a cloud. Good for children.
Into the Deep	Synthesizer with ocean sounds.	Good for all ages and sleeping issues.
Maiden Voyage	Synthesizer with nature and water sounds.	Good for all ages and sleeping issues.
Midsummer Night	Keyboards, classical guitar, nature sounds.	A walk through the woods as you gently fall into sleep. Gentle sounds.
Seaside Slumber	Solo piano, ocean waves.	Ocean sounds are very pleasing and restful. Deep restorative sleep.
Sleeping Through the Rain	Synthesizer with nature sounds including thunder.	Primarily soft dreamy music. Some of the thunder and lightning sounds have been known to be scary to younger children.
Transformation	Synthesizer.	Travel through the Chakras. Not recommended for children. Appears to have strong appeal to males.

Many users wanted to have a talk induction with the *Supersleep* Hemi-Sync®. Thus, *Restorative Sleep, Sleep, Sound Sleeper,* and *Sweet Dreams* were developed which combined an introductory visualization with the undertones of Hemi-Sync®, leading to a restful sleep. A very creative sleep aid titled *Catnapper* literally allows the brain to go in and out of a REM sleep (normally a 90-minute cycle) in a 30 minute day-time period. This is conducive to making up missed sleep in insomniacs, students, and businessmen and women. Many international travelers (and pilots) use *Catnapper* to mitigate jetlag symptoms.

More recently, because children are also experiencing increasing levels of sleep disruption, creative bedtime stories were developed with the specific sleep-state of Children's REM cycle embedded. It has been found that infants and newborns have greater needs for REM sleep than adults. Therefore, many delightful bedtime stories have been created that are appropriate for children.

TABLE 9-2: Children's Bedtime Stories with Hemi-Sync®

TITLE	DESCRIPTION	OBSERVATIONS
Angels, Fairies and Wizards	Enchanting story about a guardian angel.	Good for special needs children as well. Also available in Spanish.
Joy Jumper	Children joy jump to their favorite places.	For children having trouble falling asleep at night.
Milton's Secret	Eckhart Tolle's popular children's book based on the Power of Now.	Teaches kids how to live in the present.
Robbie the Rabbit	A journey into the forest world with sounds of nature.	Comforting and soothing.
Sleepy Locust	Bedtime story about Big Freddy outwitting the locusts.	Guides children into deep and restful sleep.
Turtle Island	American Indian story of creation.	Teaches children the importance of honoring Mother Earth. Sleep enhancement.
A Unicorn Named Georgia	Story about a Unicorn with a golden horn.	Leads children into deep and restful sleep.

Musical Relaxation and Stress Management

With the growing popularity of Metamusic®, many people find they enjoy using it for relaxation, deep relaxation, use in the background with body work, and for general release of the stress of the day. Certain music has been found to elevate healing forces in the physical body. Psychiatrist John Diamond M.D. explores the relationship between music and health in his book, *The Life Energy in Music*. In it, he notes that at some point 95 percent of the population will suffer from low thymus levels and fatigue. The thymus gland is a master gland which directs the immune response of the body. Low thymus activity can be instantly raised by listening to enhancing and soothing music. Diamond suggests that music can increase T-cell (Thymus-cell) production to five times current levels, and raise endorphin levels up to 90 times normal levels. This can improve resistance to illness, dampen the perception of pain, and evoke faster recovery times. Much of the music created for Metamusic® focuses on the harmonic tones that facilitate this healing response from the body.[102]

Why are we moved by music? Larry Dossey, M.D., says that, "One reason may be that the body itself is intrinsically musical, right down to the DNA that makes up our genes."[103] The idea that DNA and music might be connected originates with the work of Dr. Susumu Ohno, a geneticist at the Beckman Institute of the City of Hope Hospital in Duarte, California. Dr. Ohno has notated more than 15 songs based on the DNA of a variety of living organisms. He finds that the more evolved an organism, the more complicated the music. For example, the DNA of a single-cell protozoan translates into a simple four-note repetition while music transcribed from human DNA (such as the body's receptor site for insulin) is much more complex. As Dr. Ohno describes,

> Listeners knowledgeable about classical music hear similarities between these DNA-based compositions and the music of Bach, Brahms, Chopin, and other great composers. DNA melodies are majestic and inspiring. Many persons hearing them for the first time are moved to tears. They cannot believe that their bodies, which they believed to be mere collections of chemicals, contain such uplifting, inspiring harmonies—are musical.[104]

Not only can music be created starting with the DNA, it is also possible to reverse the process, that is, take a piece of music and assign nucleotides to the notes. The end result resembles a strand of DNA. Ohno tried this with a Chopin funeral march and the final result resembled a cancer gene! As Bullard sums up when lecturing,

> I believe each of our organs is singing its own song. We are healthy when our organs are singing in harmony. We feel sick when they are singing out of tune.

From my own experiences it is clear that listening to music and Metamusic® helps the body stay in tune.

A major reason Metamusic® is so powerful is the influence of the auditory nerve to the brain/body. German jazz theorist Joachim-Ernst Berendt had an epiphany with music that inspired him to research the world's religions to learn how music and sound affect the consciousness. He shared his findings in *The World is Sound—Nada Brahma* which devoted special attention to musicians like those at TMI who are composing "the new music of transformation."[105]

TABLE 9-3: Selected Metamusic® Titles for Relaxation and Stress Management

TITLE	DESCRIPTION	OBSERVATIONS
Chakra Journey	Keyboards, chimes, wind instruments.	Good for yoga and experiencing Chi. Aligns chakras.
Graceful Passages	Variety of musical forms. Includes spoken messages.	Tranquility and reflection
Hemi-Sync® Support for Healing	Classical string	Supports recuperation and well-being.
Himalayan Soul	Flute, mystical sounds.	Inner tranquility.
The Lotus Mind	Synthesizer with Asian theme.	Opening the mind and heart.
Octaves of Light	Synthesizer. Native American influence. Nature sounds.	Supports the benefits of energy and body work.
Reflections	Synthesizer and nature field recordings.	Heightens healing connection.
River Dawn	Solo piano.	Heart-felt emotion; reduces stress.
Timeless	Solo piano.	Deep relaxation; restorative state of inner peace.
Waves of Love	Electronic Keyboard. Includes ocean sounds.	Heart centered; inspired by dolphins.

Musicians and readers were particularly inspired by his chapter "The Temple is the Ear," which explores the overwhelming importance of the auditory nerve and the influence of healing music on consciousness and health. In it, Berendt points to radiological studies of MRIs which demonstrate that the auditory nerve has three times as many connections to the brain as vision does.[106] It is also the first organ to develop its full size in utero, and is the brain's greatest supplier of sensory energy. The auditory nerve through the Vagus Nerve/the 10th Cerebral nerve, connects to every major organ in the body with direct connections with the Thymus gland which connects our immune response.

TABLE 9-4: Selected Hemi-Sync® Titles for Relaxation and Stress Management

TITLE	DESCRIPTION	OBSERVATIONS
Deep 10 Relaxation	Includes both verbal guidance track and non-verbal sleep support track.	Blissful state of total relaxation followed by natural, restful sleep.
Energy Walk	Verbal guidance.	Taps natural sources of energy for healing.
Healing Journey's Support	Verbal expertise by Patty Avalon to take control of healing process (4 CDs)	Body Harmony, Chakra Tune-up, Helping Healers, Heart Energy
Hemi-Sync® Relaxation	Verbally guided by Dr. Norm Shealy	Progressive relaxation.
Journey Through the T-Cells	Guided imagery.	Stimulates T-Cell production for healing.
Pain Management	Verbal guidance.	Helps reduce pain signals.
Passages	Human Plus series.	Balances hormones and promotes positive life changes.
Positive Immunity Program (9 CDs)	Includes guided imagery and some Human Plus.	Strengthens total healing process; boosts natural immune system.
Surgical Support Series (6 CDs)	Includes guided imagery and some Human Plus.	Fosters healing and supports wellness.
Tune-up	Human Plus.	Reinforce body's natural ability to heal.

* * * * *

With our eyes we are always at the edge of the world looking in, but with our ears the world comes to us and we are always at the center of it.
-Murray Schafer

Our ears are the organ of transcendence and the gateway to the soul.
-Joachim-Ernst Berendt

* * * * *

Clearly the impact of the auditory nerve connections to the brain and the body and the implications of DNA music give us greater understanding of the impact of music. When Hemi-Sync® is added to relaxing music, the synergy can greatly augment this power. The synchronized flow of brainwave frequencies across the corpus callosum and throughout the entire brain in response to neuronal stimulation by music and Hemi-Sync® has a greater chance of stimulating the trophotropic state—the body's innate healing state.[107]

Meditation

Meditation traditions are centuries old. Yet modern science has begun to document the relaxation response and the numerous beneficial aspects of meditation. Although there are many types, meditation involves quieting the body and mind by focusing attention on a single source of unchanging input. Many forms of meditation are suggested as a pathway to rebalancing the body/mind as well as opening the doorway to deeper consciousness levels.

Researchers at the Irvine Medical Center University of California found that the practice of Transcendental Meditation (TM) actually increased the flow of blood to both hemispheres of the brain by 65 percent more than participants who were merely relaxed. This greater flow of blood supply may count in part for the many studies that show meditation improves mental performance and IQ levels up to five IQ points in two years. Meditation has also been found to be very beneficial to overall health and happiness. Fortune Magazine reported in August of 1988 that "People over 40 who spent 20 minutes twice a day meditating had 74 percent fewer doctor visits, 69 percent fewer hospital admissions than a control group who did not." However, many people seek meditation more as a consciousness expanding tool and because of a desire to achieve Oneness with a higher self.

Metamusic®, with long moments of silence for many, helps experience this sense of Oneness. For example, the use of *Inner Journey*, *Higher* and *Ascension* (just to name a few) often set the stage for enhanced meditative experiences.

When attempting to meditate with Metamusic®, finding the right Metamusic® is just the first step. To truly make the most of the listening experience, the individual must also be willing to fully participate in the process by surrendering to the *intent* of the music. Constance Demby, a well-respected symphonic space musician, explains that for the music to take you to soul levels you must be a willing participant. She encourages listeners to participate in *frontal* listening, as opposed to background listening. She says,

Ask to be taken to the same realms that the music came from ... Open your heart, surrender, and let the music in all the way. People can go much further when they consciously focus on the music and surrender to it. By allowing their minds to follow the music they are led to the Source of the music—and its transformational power. In a sense, it means meditating with the music.[108]

Many of the musicians that create music for Metamusic® understand this deeper driving force. For example, Micah Sadigh, M.D., the composer of *Inner Journey* (cover pictured earlier), *Transformation* (cover pictured earlier)*, The Visitation* and other offerings, describes this transformative interpretation from source in the following way:

Every piece I've written has had a spiritual component. It's not just "pretty" or "entertaining" music. Its purpose is to touch something deep within the listener, because I believe in the depth and mystery of humanity. My best efforts stimulate the generation and further enhancement of the listener's own images—often resulting in the discovery of something new within. In that sense, it is truly interactive music. Finally, I've realized that "my music" is not mine at al—it flows through me rather than being generated by me.[109]

Sadigh's most recent releases, *The Journey Home* and *Portal to Eternity*, continue this tradition.

J. S. Epperson, a prolific composer, sees the process of creating Metamusic® as a journey itself. He describes this journey as one of revelation, a communication of knowledge to the listener. In his words, "I hear the faint echo of a what is or what is to be and it is my journey to reveal this echo to others." He is reminded of Michelangelo's words (paraphrased), that in every block of marble there is a statue as plain as though it stood before you, shaped and perfect in attitude and action. You have only to hew away the rough walls that imprison the lovely apparition to reveal it to the other's eyes as you see it.[110]

* * * * *

Metamusic® is a journey within. It is an exploration of an inner landscape
that unfolds as you reveal yourself to you. As you listen to Metamusic®,
there is a narrative quality that plays itself out on the stage of your mind.
While it may be a beautiful story, ultimately Metamusic® has a purpose and a lesson:
it guides you along the path of self discovery.

-J. S. Epperson, Composer

* * * * *

As a rule, Metamusic® selections used for meditation have slower rhythms and melodies with periods of long chords that allow people to surf to deeper consciousness levels.

TABLE 9-5: Selected Metamusic® Titles for Meditation

TITLE	DESCRIPTION	OBSERVATIONS
Angel Paradise	Irish harp	Angelic compositions that touch the emotions of humanity.
Ascension	Transcendent synthesizer music	Music of the spheres to commune with higher aspects of Self.
Beyond the Golden Light	Synthesizer and guitar	Explores the outer reaches of consciousness.
Deep Journeys	Synthesizer	Uplifting meditative music.
Higher	Synthesizer	Ethereal tones that focus inward to the source of creation.
Inner Journey	Synthesizer.	Ethereal landscape for personal exploration.
The Journey Home	Synthesizer	Celestial music beyond space and time.
Mystic Realms	Synthesizer	Experience transcendent stillness within.
Radiance	Synthesizer, flute, angelic choir	Meditation frequencies to transport you to soul levels.

Shamanic Journey

Whereas many people seek higher consciousness states through meditation, others seek expanded awareness through closer connection to Mother Earth, or GAIA, and enjoy the Shamanic practices that have emerged from indigenous cultures all over the world.

Metamusic® for relaxation, sleep and bodywork is more gentle and focused on long chords of silence; Shamanic Metamusic® is very active, with lots of sounds to grab the attention and drive consciousness. Listeners to the many Metamusic® selections that are termed "Shamanic" need to understand that they focus on drumming, rattles, conches, flutes, didgeridoo, bird calls and other nature sounds to evoke the whole range of earth connections. Because of this dynamic variety of sounds, some people choose to use the Shamanic Metamusic® during daytime journeys into expanded consciousness.

The younger generations appear to have a deep appreciation and desire for this style of Metamusic®. The drumming (and rhythmic dancing) that are part of

Shamanic Metamusic® seeks to cultivate the important entrainment needed between the head and the heart. This entrainment can not only increase expanded states of consciousness, a sense of Oneness, but also improve health.

There are a variety of Metamusic® offerings that are in the genre of Shamanism. Most of these offerings are more recent in response to expressed desires of the Net Generation, many of whom participate in tribal-based gatherings in their search for expanded consciousness. Most of the Shamanic Metamusic® is performed by well-known musicians who brought their music to TMI for the express purpose of embedding underlying Hemi-Sync® tones to create a greater synergy of response and impact.

Because of the success of Shamanic Metamusic®, one of the leading Metamusic® composers created an expanded Shamanic experience for The Monroe Institute based on his single Metamusic® offering. *The Shaman's Heart* program uses a combination of music and sound, meditation, personal intention, specially created Hemi-Sync® sessions, HoloShamanic Breathwork, and integrative processing. HoloShamanic Breathwork is a strategy for directly contacting the intrinsic healing power within each individual. Developed by Byron Metcalf, Ph.D., this unique approach combines key components from Grof's Holotropic Breathwork™ with various shamanic healing methods that have been used since the dawn of recorded history. As a drummer, percussionist and recording engineer, Byron produces music for deep inner exploration, breathwork, shamanic journeywork, body-oriented therapies, various meditation practices and the healing arts.

The Shaman's Heart is award-winning Metamusic®. In a review of *The Shaman's Heart* by Bill Binkelman, editor of *Wind and Wire*, he stated, "My mind boggles at the idea this was created in the studio, as it almost feels like it emerged new born from the very heart of the jungle itself. There is little else to say except WOW!"

TABLE 9-6: Selected Shamanic Metamusic®

TITLE	DESCRIPTION	OBSERVATIONS
Between Worlds	Didgeridoo, flutes, synthesizer.	Journey through the rain forest.
Breath of Creation	Holy breath through fired clay flute.	Primal sound journey.
Deep Time Dreaming	Drums, clay pots, overtones.	A portal of Shamanic travel. (Recognized by Backroads Records as the number one release in 2003 of all genres.)
Dream Catcher	Synthesizer, water sounds, drones.	Soothing ambient music.
The Dreaming Gate	Didgeridoo, Tibetan horns, cello, drums, vocals/chants.	Tribal music of Inlakesh.
Dream Seed	Didgeridoo, synthesizer, drums, crystal singing bowls, flutes.	Accesses the healing energy within.
Egyptian Sun	Middle Eastern music: tablas, drums, keyboards and chants.	A journey to the Egyptian pyramids and temples.
GAIA	Flute and guitar, sounds of water.	A musical journey of Kokopelli.
The Shaman's Heart	Drums, didgeridoo, Shamanic rattles.	Traveling the Shamanic path with the heart.
Spirit Gathering	Drums, flutes, synthesizer, nature sounds.	Primordial Shamanic journey.
Star Spirits	Native flutes, synthesizer, drums and nature sounds.	Sounds of the night deepen the Native American journey.
Tribal Journeys	Berimbau, percussion, drumming.	Ancient African instruments create an other-worldly state.
Vision Quest	Drums, percussion, shakers and synthesizer.	Surrounded by tribal elders, your vision quest begins.
Where the Earth Touches the Stars	Instruments, native flutes and synthesizers.	Music that is grounded in the earth yet connected to the stars.
Winds Over the World	Aboriginal flutes, wind.	An Aboriginal Journey to peace and calm.

Chapter 10

Remembrance of the Journey
(a story)

The classroom was empty. Well, not literally, perhaps, all the regulars were there student-wise, just no teacher. Where was she? Was class called off? **R**enee, sitting right up front like always, glanced again at her watch, then looked around at **E**leanor (who liked to be called Ellie), sitting one row back to the right. "This is unusual," she whispered, then realized it didn't really matter if she whispered. So she cleared her throat and added a bit louder, "Really unusual!"

In the back of the room **M**averick—no doubt a nickname, but no one knew any other name to call him—was humming as he looked out the side windows, appearing totally oblivious to the fact that the clock was ticking away without Professor B standing at the front of the room, without the class agenda written on the front board, and without the welcoming Metamusic® of the day playing softly in the background. Maverick was probably the most artistic of the group, although several other students had demonstrated latent drawing talents during the semester. When the class was exploring the power of self-affirmations Maverick had come up with what he called the *eternal triangle* visual representing the self-concept (I am), the self-image (I see) and self-esteem (I feel). Everyone benefited, with the visual finding its way through classroom after classroom across the campus. Pretty impressive. While Maverick always *appeared* disengaged in class, as was the case now, he was *fully* engaged.

"Okay," boomed a low female voice from the left of the room. "Who's going to take responsibility for the class? I can't afford to miss another one, and really made an effort to be here. So, let's do something." It was **E**manita.

A cacophony of voices responded.

"Professor B is always saying we can teach ourselves."

"What are we supposed to do?"

"How about we review for the final?"

"What does the syllabus say for this class?"

"We're supposed to prepare for the exam."

"**M**ary should take the lead."

"Let's all contribute."

"This is a communications class. How about we communicate?"

Picking her name out from the chorus, Mary stood and walked to the front. Mary was, after all, on the student council. "Quiet, everyone, one person at a time. How about we let the majority rule? First, how many of you want to stay and create our own class?" A good three fourths of the class raised their hand. "I'm impressed," Mary laughed. "You guys must like this class as much as I do?"

"Why?" came the small voice of **B**renda sitting near the middle in the third row back.

"Why what?"

"Why do you like this class?"

Mary was a bit taken back, but quickly regrouped. "Okay, that's a good starting point. Only let's make it a *what* question: What do we like about what we've been learning? That question will help us review for the exam next week. And as we share, let's each pretend we're the one up front so we practice our presentation skills. Who wants to start?"

Maverick stood and walked toward the front.

"I thought you were watching out the window," Mary chided. Aside from their names both starting with an "M", Maverick and Mary had a special relationship, having dated for a short while earlier in the year.

"You know I hear everything," Maverick hissed back quietly, then motioned Mary gently into a chair at the front of the room, and took center stage. He seemed to expand, actually grow larger, and the presence that began speaking in strong confident tones was NOT the spacey classroom Maverick!

"I'd like to share with you what I have learned about the power of visualization," Maverick began. The classroom fell silent. This was something that Maverick knew about; and by gosh with exams looming it just might be a good idea to listen to him.

In a hush they waited. And waited. Finally, Rahim asked the silent Maverick what he was planning on saying.

"Nothing," answered Maverick. "My presence has just said it. It's all in my right brain, and that doesn't speak. It is visual." Maverick bowed to the clapping of hands and glided to his seat, sustaining his expanded state. Mary was up on her feet quickly, looking around for the next volunteer. But all heads were turned toward Maverick, who now was slumped in his chair staring out the window.

"Any volunteers?" Mary asked. The heads turned back her direction, but no one moved to raise a hand. "Hmmm ..." Mary mumbled. "I guess it's my turn. I brought a surprise for all of you, although I didn't imagine the context of giving it out!" She pulled out a pile of stapled groups of paper.

"How many trees did you kill?" came from **R**ahim off to the side.

"If you don't want it, you don't need to take it," Mary said defiantly. "These are my notes from the whole semester, and there's a copy for each of you."

Rahim quickly recanted. "Hey, I can use paper almost as well as the Internet." He sat smiling. "And I missed a few classes, so your notes might prove quite handy." Others chimed in agreement.

Mary carefully counted out the grouped papers, making sure to take her time, and gave a stack to each person sitting in the front row to pass backward. Then she took her place center front. "So, a quick review. First, attitudes toward learning." [Chapter 2]

Renee read from the notes in front of her: "*Have a proactive attitude towards the importance of learning.*"

"That's right," Mary answered, "Now let's see if we can remember rather than read the notes.

From Eleanor, "There's one about *knowing that you can do it.* Remember the anecdote Antoine shared about Henry Ford?" **A**ntoine, who had been relatively quiet until now, spoke up, "If you think you can or you think you can't you're right!" A murmur of voices agreed.

"That's where visualization and affirmation can come in handy," chimed in a voice from the back.

"True," Mary agreed. "We'll get to that in a minute."

"Next is the bit about *have fun and being excited about all the stuff around us we can learn*," boomed in **Noah**, who had one of those baritone voices you knew was going to be something neat or weird like a radio announcer or opera singer!

"*And choosing to learn* is part of that one," added Rahim.

"Next is *looking for the relevance to your own life of what you are learning*," said Jean, clearly peeking at her notes again.

"Let's not forget the part about *choosing a time and place that will help you have sustained focus on what you are doing*," chimed in Emanita.

"And," added Antoine with a sigh of finality, "*keeping a positive eye on the end goal*."

"There's that visualizing again," chimed in the voice from the back.

"Remember the fun we had creating metaphors?" asked John, another silent party, but no more. "I wrote one about being a video camera."

"I was a piece of blank paper," added Renee.

Mary took the lead again. "We really did quite well on that. How about *Samantic Realignment*?" [Chapter 3]

"That means *being more conscientious and aware of the verbal programming we are inputting into our left brain*," said Maverick, with his face still turned toward the window and his eyes trained on the tree just beyond.

"Things like *eliminating the negative and destructive words* we use to describe ourselves as a learner and *replacing them with positive energizing, and more life-affirming word choices*." From Renee. Was she reading the notes again?

"How about an example?" asked Mary.

"It's like not saying we stink at this, but saying we're really good and getting better!" from Rahim. There was laughter.

"Let's remember the two keys to Semantic Realignment, Brenda stated. "(1) *to use verbs which indicate action followed by positive qualifiers*; and (2) *to only use positive nouns in our speech*." It didn't look like she was reading the notes.

"Now can we talk about affirmations?" came the voice from the back.

"Yeah, remember the neat affirmations we created as a homework assignment?" said **Nitesh**, actively joining the dialogue underway, a rare event for this quiet reflective soul. "We were able to *supercharge our brain rewiring with affirmations*!" Emanita wondered what supercharging Nitesh's brain rewiring would be like. She'd known him a long time, and always liked him, but had only heard him speak on rare occasionally. One time was when he was the valedictorian at their high school graduation (and she had no doubt he would continue that pattern when they graduated from college!) Just maybe she should try harder to get closer to him. A supercharged Nitesh might just mean another Steve Jobs!

"Is it time to talk more about visualization?" asked the voice from the back.

"We have a step-by-step process for crafting creative visualizations," said Mary, opening her notes. "Why not write them up on the board?" [Chapter 4]

Carol got up and went to the board. She was silent as she picked up the chalk, then turned to capture the input from the class. She was one of those budding artists.

"*Having the right frame of mind*, I mean, *being relaxed*, maybe *closing your eyes*, in a *quiet place*," said Eleanor.

"And creating a plot, just like a script for a move," added Renee, NOT looking at the notes.

Then **E**sther popped into the conversation, "Then *refining your script*, and then *creating a more vivid image* and *making sure it is interactive*."

"Next is *visualization*," came the voice from the back, "right along with *role rehearsal*." Heads turned to see who that was, but they couldn't tell. Couldn't tell whether it was a guy or girl voice either. "And to *involve as many of our five senses as we can*, letting our *imagination run freely*." Heads turned again (in vain) to find the source of the voice.

"Enter music," said Mary, as she turned a page in her notes.

"I'd like to talk about super learning, and communicating from the inside out." Nitesh stated as he took center stage. Carol sat down in silence as Nitesh continued. "This class is about communicating. I always thought that was interacting on the outside; now I know I'm communicating all the time, within me and with others, even without me knowing it! But my focus this morning is the powerful communicating from the inside out, and how we can facilitate that communication through the use of music and Metamusic®." [Chapter 5]

Maverick was expanding right out of his chair and up to the board. Now he was drawing. Everyone watched with awe as he drew a stack of twisting doors, then swirled the words "COMMUNICATING FROM THE INSIDE OUT" from underneath the doors. This is what he drew:

Meanwhile, silent Carol had been setting up her computer on Professor B's desk. She flicked her mouse and the tones of the Metamusic® *Remembrance* began playing. They all knew it, of course; it's just one of those pieces of music that creates a knowing. With the backdrop set, the group continued their exchange with Nitesh taking the lead.

"While we all know this is Metamusic® that has Hemi-Sync® under it, let's first recall the specific features of music that support learning. Who remembers?" Seven hands went up.

Esther recited: "*No lyrics, 30-40 minutes of uninterrupted music with a repeatable refrain, harmonic and rhythmic, and energized. Oh, and pick something from a "warm and fuzzy" movie rather than a horror show!*" She winked at Rahim. Something was going on there.

"Let's talk about memory aids. First in the learning space," said Nitesh. "After you *select your favorite soundtrack or preferred Baroque music*, there are other things to consider."

Esther was on a roll. "*That's doing some slow breathing, placing a distinct aroma in your study space, and adding in positive self-talk.*"

From Nitesh: "Remember the memory aid: **Music + confident attitude + breath + smell + taste.** Then the day of recall ..."

Renee read this response from the notes: "*Breathe in and out four times; allow the attitude and feelings of total confidence; imagine your eventual success; recall the smells, the taste and the musical format; and take the test with confidence and ease.*"

Nitesh summed up, "That's the whole brain approach which *helps you study smarter, not harder*, enabling super learning. *Remembrance* was in the second section now. The energy of the group was high; they didn't want to stop, but time kept moving on.

"How about we all commit to using our favorite Beta Metamusic® as we study our—and Mary's—notes? Then we could just relax for 15 minutes and enjoy *Remembrance*." This was Brenda's suggestion. The vote was unanimous, and they all reveled in the musical journey, some with heads down, others peacefully gazing and soft breathing ... something like what Maverick always appeared to be doing?

With the conclusion of *Remembrance* Carol stopped the re-loop while they all raised and stretched, something like the wave that you practice for a football game, one after the other. It started with **R**enee, then **E**leanor, **M**averick and **E**manita followed by **M**ary, **B**renda and **R**ahim. Then there was **A**ntoine and **N**itesh, and finally **C**arol and **E**sther, then all the others in one S-W-I-S-H!

They were happy with the class, and still wondering what on earth had happened to Professor B. No doubt this next week there would be some juicy gossip around campus about their unusual exam prep!

Emanita and Mary were the last ones out of class, making a point to close the door behind them. Emanita held her copy of Mary's semester notes in her right hand. Her left hand was up on her shoulder hooked around the strap of her backpack. "Couldn't you have made these more concise and shorter?" she questioned. "This is going to take a lot of work."

"Just scan them," Mary said helpfully. Since you *mind is an associative patterner*, you just need to recall all the stuff we talked about in class this semester.

"THAT won't work," Emanita retorted. "I'm the one who missed my quota of possible misses. Professor B won't forgive my absences unless I ace this exam!"

"Then I suggest you study *smarter, not harder*," Mary quickly responded, smiling. "And for goodness sakes use Metamusic®." She walked down the hall without a backward glance.

Emanita sighed. Yep, it sure was good she'd learned about the music thing. She stood there in the hall alone ... remembering the discussions about how her mind/brain worked ... remembering the power of visualization and affirmations ... remembering who she was. With *Remembrance* she could do this! Her mind's eye visualized an "A" on her exam. It was sure a good thing she'd done some meta-learning.

It was then that Emanita noticed the door across the hall wide open with Professor B coming through it into the hall. Professor B stopped, lips in one of those wide knowing smiles, and looked Emanita in the eye. "It was a great class," she confided, very matter of fact. "I'm really glad I was running late." Then with a wink she turned and strode away.

Remembrance (the Book) Endnotes

[1] Begley, S. (2007), *Train Your Mind, Change Your Brain*, Ballantine Books, New York, p. 48.

[2] Restak, R. (2003), *The New Brain: How the Modern Age is Rewiring Your Mind*, Rodale, St. Martin's Press, New York, p. 8.

[3] fMRI (functional magnetic resonance imaging) is used for neuroimaging to produce precise measurements of the brain's structure. PET (positron-emission tomography) measures the brain's consumption of energy. EEG (electroencephalograph) measures the average electrical activity of large populations of neurons. TMS (transcranial magnetic stimulation) uses head-mounted wire coils that send very short by strong magnetic pulses directly into specific brain regions that induce low-level electric currents into the brain's neural circuits. While this technology is very young, it appears to be able to turn on and off different parts of the human brain.

[4] National Science Foundation and Decade of the Brain, June 21, 1991, Report, NSF9158

[5] http://news.stanford.edu/news/2013/april/bran-project-stanford-040213.html (July 15, 2013)

[6] National Research Council (2000), *How People Learn: Brain, Mind, Experience, and School*. Washington, DC: National Academy Press, p. 5.

[7] Tapscott, D. (2009), *Grown Up Digital*, McGraw Hill, New York.

[8] Begley (2007), op.cit., p. 180.

[9] See (Gardner) http://www.howardgardner.com/MI/mi.htm and http://www.multipleintelligencetheory.co.uk/

[10] Zull, J.E. (2002), *The Art of Changing the Brain: Enriching the Practice of Teaching by Exploring the Biology of Learning*, Stylus, Sterling.

[11] Ibid. See http://www.sharpbrains.com/blog/2006/10/12/an-ape-can-do-this-can-we-not/ and http://fpdc.kent.edu/oldsite/profdev/pdf/Zull/Zull%20paperCG.pdf

[12] Ibid, p. 68. See http://www.npr.org/templates/story/story.php?storyId=7131130

[13] Byrnes, J.P. (2001), Minds, *Brains and Learning: Understanding the Psychological and Educational Relevance of Neuroscientific Research*, The Guilford Press, New York, p.181.

[14] Johnson, S. and K. Taylor (Eds.) (2006), *The Neuroscience of Adult Learning*, Jossey-Bass, San Francisco, CA., p. 7. See http://www.amazon.com/The-Neuroscience-Adult-Learning-Directions/dp/0787987042

[15] Zull (2002), op.cit., p. 209. See http://www.sharpbrains.com/blog/2006/10/12/an-ape-can-do-this-can-we-not/

[16] Bennet, A. and Bennet, D. (2006), "Learning as associative patterning", in *VINE: The Journal of Information and Knowledge Management Systems*, Vol. 36. No. 4, pp. 371-376. And,

Bennet, A. and D. Bennet (2008), "Engaging tacit knowledge in support of organizational learning", in *VINE: The Journal of Information and Knowledge Management Systems*, Vol. 40. No. 1, 2008.

[17] Pert, C. (1997), *Molecules of Emotion: The Science Behind Mind-Body Medicine*, Scribner, New York, NY.

[18] Lipton, B. (2005), *The Biology of Belief: Unleashing the Power of Consciousness, Matter and Miracles*, Elite Books, Santa Rosa, CA.

[19] Edelman, G. M. and G. Tononi (2000), *A Universe of Consciousness: How Matter Becomes Imagination*, Basic Books, New York, NY.

[20] Neji, M. and M. Ben Ammar (2007), "Emotional eLearning system", presentation to the Fourth International Conference on eLearning for Knowledge-Based Society, November 18-19, Bangkok, Thailand. See http://www.tarakbenammar.com/en

[21] Lipton (2005), op.cit.

[22] See http://www.ted.com/talks/michael_merzenich_on_the_elastic_brain.html.

[23] See https://embryo.asu.edu/pages/roger-sperrys-split-brain-experiments-1959-1968

[24] McGilchrist, Iain (2009), *The Master and His Emissary*, Yale University Press, London. See http://www.ted.com/talks/iain_mcgilchrist_the_divided_brain.html

[25] Ibid, p 27.

[26] See http://www.carlsagan.com/ and http://en.wikipedia.org/wiki/Carl_Sagan

[27] Bennet and Bennet (2008), op.cit.

[28] See http://www.peterrussell.com/index2.php

[29] See http://en.wikipedia.org/wiki/Buckminster_Fuller

and http://bfi.org/about-bucky

[30] *Ibid.*

[31] See https://www.stephencovey.com/

[32] *Ibid*, p. 33.

[33] See https://www.youtube.com/watch?v=mbJlgEyF0-w

[34] Russell, P. (2010), *The Brain Book: Know Your Own Mind and How to Use It*, Penguin Books, New York. See http://www.peterrussell.com/brainbook/brainbook.php

[35] Tapscott, D. (2009), *Grown Up Digital: How the Net Generation is Changing Your World*, McGraw-Hill, New York.

[36] Williams, L. V. (1983), *Teaching for the Two-Sided Mind: A Guide to Right Brain/Left Brain Education,* Prentice Hall, New Jersey.

[37] Bry, A. and M. Bair (1979), *Visualization: Directing the Movies of Your Mind*, Harper Perennial Library, New York.

[38] Russell (2010), op.cit.

[39] Bennet, A. and D. Bennet (2008a), "The Human Knowledge System: Music and Brain Coherence" in *VINE*, Vol. 38, No. 3, pp. 277-296.

[40] See https://en.wikipedia.org/wiki/Hero%27s_journey

[41] Ostrander, S. and L. Schroedder (1982), *Super Learning*, http://superlearning.ca/collections/books-and-publications

[42] McGilchrist (2009), op.cit. p. 3.

[43] Levy, J. (1974), "Cerebral asymmetries as manifested in split-brain man" in M. Kinsbourne & W.L. Smith (eds.), *Hemispheric disconnection and cerebral function*, Charles C. Thomas, Springfield, IL.

[44] Levitin, D.J. (2006), *This is your Brain on Music: The Science of a Human Obsession,* Penguin Group, New York.

[45] Tame, D. (1988), The Secret Power of Music: The Transformaton of Self and Society through Musical Energy, Aquarian Press, Wellingborough, U.K.

[46] See http://www.drjohndiamond.com/ and http://www.youtube.com/watch?v=ERvEMMCmmuc).

[47] Wilson, T. (2006, 3rd Printing), "Chant: the Healing Power of Voice and Ear (an interview with Alfred Tomatis)" in Campbell, D., *Music: Physician for Times to Come*, Quest Books, Wheaton, IL

[48] See http://www.personal.psu.edu/faculty/v/n/vns/

[49] The music Remembrance can be purchased from The Monroe Institute. See www.monroeinstitute.org or from www.Hemi-Sync.com

[50] See http://www.monroeinstitute.org/

[51] This is offered on the Gaia channel on Amazon.

[52] Bennet, A. and D. Bennet (2007), *Knowledge Mobilization in the Social Sciences and Humanities: Moving from Research to Action*, MQI Press, Frost, WV.

[53] Oster, G. (1973), "Auditory beats in the brain", *Scientific American*, 229, pp. 94-102.39.

[54] See http://www.binauralblog.com/?p=62

[55] Oster, (1973), ob.cit.

[56] Swann, R., S. Bosanko, R. Cohen, R., R. Midgley and K.M. Seed (1982), *The Brain: A User's Manual*, G.P. Putnam & Sons, New York, NY.

[57] Hink, R.F., K. Kodera, O. Yamada, K. Kaga, and J. Suzuki (1980), "Binaural interaction of a beating frequency following response", *Audiology*, 19, pp. 36-43.

Marsh, J.T., W.S. Brown, and J.C. Smith (1975), "Far-field recorded frequency-following responses: correlates of low pitch auditory perception in humans", *Electroencephalography and Clinical Neurophysiology*, 38, pp. 113-119.

Smith, J.C., J.T. Marsh, S. Greenberg, and W.S. Brown (1978), "Human auditory frequency-following responses to a missing fundamental", *Science*, 201, pp. 639-641.

[58] Ritchey, D. (2003), *The H.I.S.S. of the A.S.P.: Understanding the Anomalously Sensitive Person*, Headline Books, Inc., Terra Alta, WV.

[59] Carroll, G. D. (1986), "Brain hemisphere synchronization and musical learning", reprint of paper published by University of North Carolina at Greensboro, NC.

[60] Atwater, F.H. (2004), *The Hemi-Sync Process*, The Monroe Institute, Faber, VA.

Fischer, R. (1971), "A cartography of ecstatic and meditative states", *Science*, 174 (4012), pp. 897-904. Delmonte, M.M. (1984), "Electrocortical activity and related phenomena associated with meditation practice: A literature review", in *International Journal of Neuroscience*, 24, pp. 217-231.

Goleman, G.M. (1988), *Meditative Mind: The Varieties of Meditative Experience*, G.P. Putnam, New York, NY. Jevning, R., R.K. Wallace, and M. Beidenbach (1992), "The physiology of meditation: A review", *Neuroscience and Behavioral Reviews*, 16, pp. 415-424. Mavromatis, A. (1991), *Hypnagogia*, Routledge, New York, NY. West, M.A. (1980), "Meditation and the EEG", *Psychological Medicine*, 10, pp. 369-375.

[61] Schwartz, S.A. (1998), "The Path of Sound" in *Intuition*, September/October.

[62] Casey, Ginger (1991) in *TMI Focus*, Winter, p. 4.

[63] See http://www.new-vis.com/ and http://www.innerpeacemusic.com/

[64] Mikaomi Usui of Kyoto, Japan, is credited with rediscovering this energy form of healing near the end of the 19th century. It is he who named this energy *Rei-Ki*. The character *Rei* in Japanese translates into *energy, nature, talent and feeling*. When combined with *Ki* (the essential life force), the term *Reiki* is translated as *universal life energy*.

[65] Carter, Gari (1993), *Healing Myself: A Hero's Primer for Recovery from Tragedy*, Hampton Roads Publishing, Charlottesville, VA

[66] See http://www.neuroacoustic.com/ and http://www.brainsync.com/

[67] Sornson, R.O. (1999), "Using Binaural Beats to Enhance Attention" in *Hemi-Sync Journal*, Vol XVII, No. 4.

[68] See http://www.russellbarkley.org/

[69] See http://www.amenclinics.com/

[70] Bullard, B. (2003), "METAMUSIC: Music for Inner Space" in *Hemi-Sync Journal*, Summer/Fall.

[71] Bennet, A. and D. Bennet (2009), "The Human Knowledge System: Music and Brain Coherence" in *Hemi-Sync Journal*, Summer/Fall. Also as Appendix B in this book.

[72] Sornson (1999), op.cit.

[73] See http://www.higher-music.com

[74] Sornson (1999), op.cit.

[75] Davis, D.D. (1996), "Oh, the Stories I Could Tell: Hemi-Sync® in Family Therapy" in *Hemi-Sync Journal*, Winter.

[76] Davis (1996), op.cit.

[77] *Ibid.*

[78] *Brain Mind Bulletin* (1990), Interface Press, Los Angeles.

[79] Rauscher, F.H., G.L. Shaw, and K.N. Ky (1993), "Music and spatial task performance", *Nature*, 365, p. 611.

[80] Rideout, B.E. and C.M. Laubach, (1996), "EEG correlates of enhanced spatial performance following exposure to music", *Perceptual & Motor Skills*, 2, pp. 427-432. Also, Rideout, B.E. and J. Taylor (1997), "Enhanced spatial performance following 10 minutes exposure to music: A replication", *Perceptual & Motor Skills*, 85, pp. 112-114. Also, Rideout, B.E., S. Dougherty and L. Wernert (1998), "Effect of music on spatial performance: A test of generality", *Perceptual & Motor Skills*, 86, pp. 512-514. And, Wilson, T.L. and T.L. Brown (1997), "Reexamination of the effect of Mozart's music on spatial-task performance", *Journal of Psychology,* 13, pp. 365-370.

[81] Steele, K.M., J.D. Brown, and J.A. Stoecker (1999), "Failure to confirm the Raushcer and Shaw description of recovery of the Mozart effect", *Perceptual & Motor Skills* 88, pp. 843-849. Also, Chabris, C. (1999), "A quantitative meta-analysis of Mozart studies", *Nature*, 400, pp. 826-827.

[82] Muftuler, L.T., M. Bodner, G.L. Shaw, and O. Nalcioglu (1999), "fMRI of Mozart effect using auditory stimuli", abstract presented at the 87th meeting of the International Society for Magnetic Resonance in Medicine, Philadelphia.

[83] Johnson, J.D.; C.W. Cotman, C.S. Tasaki, and G.L. Shaw (1998), "Enhancement of spatial-temporal reasoning after a Mozart listening condition in Alzheimer's disease: A case study", *Neurology Research* 20, pp. 666-672.

[84] Hughes, J.R., J.J. Fino, and M.A. Melyn (1999), "Is there a chronic change of the 'Mozart effect' on epileptiform activity? A case study", *Clinical Electroenceph.* 30, pp. 44-45.

[85] Felix, U. (1993), "The contribution of background music to the enhancement of learning in suggestopedia: A critical review of the literature", *Journal of the Society for Accelerative Learning and Teaching*, 18.3-4, pp. 277-303.

[86] Jensen, E. (2000b), *Brain-Based Learning: The New Science of Teaching & Training*, The Brain Store, San Diego, CA.

[87] King, J. (1991), "Comparing alpha induction differences between two music samples", abstract from the Center for Research on Learning and Cognition, University of North Texas, TX.

[88] Lozanov, G. (1991), "On some problems of the anatomy, physiology and biochemistry of cerebral activities in the global-artistic approach in modern sugestopedagogic training", *The Journal of the Society for Accelerative Learning and Teaching* 16.2, pp. 101-16.

[89] Clynes, M. (Ed.) (1982), *Music, Mind and Brain*, Plenum Press, New York, NY.

[90] See http://www.learningdoorway.com/georgi-lozanov.html

[91] See
http://www.boston.com/news/globe/obituaries/articles/2005/05/02/gordon_shaw_his_work_led_to_mozart_effect_learning_theory/?page=full

[92] Ramo, J.C. (1993), "Mozart and Intelligence Essays" in *Newsweek*, October 25, (3255 13).

[93] See http://www.higher-music.com

[94] See http://thepowerofsound.net/

95 See http://www.innerpeacemusic.com/

[96] Certo, Mark (1990), *TMI Focus*, Spring, p. 4.

[97] *LA Times*, Monday, November 3, 2008, p. F3.

[98] See https://www.nhlbi.nih.gov/grants-and-training/funding-opportunities-and-contacts/sleep-science-disorders

[99] Monroe, R. (1991), TMI Focus, Vol. XIII, No. 3, p. 2.

[100] Hobson, A.J. (1994), "Sleep and the Immune System" in *The Chemistry of Conscious States; How the Brain Changes Its Mind*, New York: Little, Brown & Co.

[101] See http://en.wikipedia.org/wiki/Allan_Hobson

[102] See http://www.drjohndiamond.com/the-works-of-john-diamond-md/23-the-life-energy-in-music-three-volume-series

[103] Dossey, L. (1992), "Your Body is Music" in Campbell, D., *Music and Miracles*, D. Campbell, Los Angeles: Quest Books, p. 55-56.

[104] Dossey (1992), op.cit., p. 56-57. See http://en.wikipedia.org/wiki/Susumu_Ohno

[105] Berendt, J-E. (1991), The World is Sound: Nada Brahma: Music and the Landscape of Consciousness, Destiny Books, Boston, MA.

[106] Berendt (1991), op.cit.

[107] Downloaded in 2003 under Healing, Peak Experiences, and the Ergotropic and Trophotropic systems, Thelaceweb-healing ourselves and the world (no longer accessible).

[108] Personal email to Barbara Bullard, 2003. See http://www.constancedemby.com/

[109] Sadigh, M. (1994) quoted in *TMI Focus*, Vol. XVI, No. 4, Fall.

[110] See http://higher-music.com/

Appendix A

eLearning as energetic learning

Alex Bennet and David Bennet

Abstract

Purpose—This paper explores the role of emotion in learning, specifically, eLearning and its relationship to the phenomenon called energetic learning.

Design/methodology/approach—After first presenting operation definitions, we look through the lens of new findings in neuroscience to build an understanding of the role of emotions in learning. We then focus specifically on how eLearning systems contribute to energetic learning, providing examples of eLearning platforms and software programs currently available that have specific attributes contributing to energetic learning.

Findings—With technology comes a natural excitement in terms of connectivity and its support of self-driven, experiential learning which is part of our evolutionary heritage. As our understanding of the neuroscience and biology of human learning advances, we are beginning to better understand the personal needs of individual learners. Bringing these needs together with eLearning system capabilities will offer a significant jump in our learning rate and efficiency as we move into a future filled with change, uncertainty, complexity and anxiety.

Keywords: energetic learning, eLearning, emotion, eLearning systems, knowledge, brain, complex adaptive system

Introduction

eLearning systems are playing a leading role in both informal continuous learning and formal education structures in the business and academic communities. In the national report of online learning, *Learning in the 21st Century*, one out of three students selected online classes as a component of their ideal school and 77 percent of teachers believe that technology makes a difference in learning. While increased choices, flexibility, and connectivity certainly contribute to these findings, there is also a leveling that emotionally engages the learner. The report concluded that as online learning becomes integrated into the day-to-day lives of individuals, there is a break-down of the compartmentalization of education. "Everyone becomes a learner and an expert with opportunities to seek and share what they know, critique what they learn, and become more engaged and involved with the global community" (Netday and Blackboard, 2006). Thus learning becomes part of everyday work (and play) and moves from a "push" model to a "pull" model driven by individual choices.

We begin this exploration with an operational definition of knowledge. Recognizing the important role that emotions play in all learning, we then introduce the concept of energetic learning and explore the ways that eLearning can support and enhance energetic learning. Next, we focus on eLearning systems in support of personalized learning. As technology continues to exponentially advance, the adaptivity and robustness of eLearning become feasible and powerful attributes that can satisfy the specific needs and idiosyncrasies of individual learners. Simultaneously, as our understanding of neuroscience and the biology of human learning advances, we are beginning to better understand the personal needs of individual learners. Bringing these needs together with eLearning system capabilities can accelerate our learning rate and efficiency as we move into a future filled with change, uncertainty, complexity and anxiety.

Setting the Stage

Embracing Stonier's description of information as a basic property of the Universe—as fundamental as matter and energy (Stonier, 1992; Stonier, 1997)—we take information to be the result of organization expressed as any non-random pattern or set of patterns. Data (a subset of information) would then be simple patterns, and while data and information are both patterns, they would have no meaning until some organism recognized and interpreted those patterns. In other words, meaning comes from the combination of non-random patterns and an observer who can interpret these patterns to create a message (Bennet and Bennet, 2007). It is only when the incoming patterns from the environment are integrated with the internal neural patterns within the brain that they take on meaning to an individual. These units of understanding are referred to as semantic complexes.

When considering learning and knowledge, neuronal patterns offer a useful perspective (Stonier, 1997). As a high-level description, knowledge exists in the human brain in the form of stored or expressed neural patterns that may be activated and reflected upon through conscious thought. As a broad, operational (functional) definition, *knowledge can be considered the capacity (potential or actual) to take effective action in varied and uncertain situations* (Bennet and Bennet, 2004). Note that use of this functional definition points to knowledge as a creation of the human mind since computers (at least for the present) cannot be programmed to deal with varied and uncertain circumstances.

Knowledge is composed of two parts: Knowledge (Informing) and Knowledge (Proceeding) (Bennet and Bennet, 2008). This builds on the distinction made by Ryle (1949) between "knowing that" and "knowing how". Knowledge (Informing), or Kn_I, is the *information* part of knowledge, representing insights, meaning, understanding, expectations, theories and principles that support or lead to effective action. When these are viewed separately they are information; when used as part of the knowledge process they are considered knowledge. Knowledge (Proceeding), or Kn_P, represents the *process and action* part of knowledge, the process of selecting information from a situation at hand (and its environment) and mixing it with internal information to develop new information patterns that guide and drive effective action.

Building on our definition of knowledge, learning is considered the *creation* or *acquisition* of the ability (potential or actual) for people to take effective action. From a neuroscientific perspective, this means that learning is the identification, selection and mixing of the relevant neural patterns (information) within the learner's mind with the information from the situation and its environment to create understanding, meaning and anticipation of the results of selected actions. The term *energetic learning* borrows from the formal definition of Energetics, the scientific study of energy flows and storages under transformation (Wikipedia, 2008). At the individual level, energetic learning is considered a state of *high energy flow* within the brain of an individual who is very interested, perhaps passionate, about a specific learning phenomenon, situation or process or an area or field of study; and/or energized, excited, confident, open and desirous of creating and exploring new ideas. Emotion is foundational to learning. As Johnson and Taylor (2006) explain, "The chemicals of emotion act by modifying the strength and contribution of each part of the learning cycle. Their impact is directly on the signaling systems in each affected neuron" (p. 7). This is the essence of energetic learning.

While electronic learning (eLearning) could be considered any virtual act or process used to acquire data or information, or to create knowledge, when the term is used today it is most often in the context of computer-based learning support systems, and periodically associated with advanced distributed learning technology. Energetic learning and eLearning are both physical experiences; energetic learning in the sense of chemically-induced positive emotions attached to the process of learning or the content of the learning, and eLearning in terms of the learner's involvement with technology. Both energetic learning and eLearning deal with patterns; energetic learning in the sense of patterns in the brain complexing with incoming patterns and cascading up and down in hierarchical relationships, and eLearning in terms of the patterns of bits and bytes presented as visual and audible information to the learner. Both energetic learning and eLearning are experiential learning and, as explicated below, are quite compatible. Ideally, good eLearning would facilitate an experience with the learner that creates emotional tags, thus enhancing the ability to learn from that experience. This is discussed further below.

An *eLearning system* encompasses and integrates critical learning conditions such as feedback, re-enforcers, motivators and information sources that enable learning to occur (Salomon and Perkins, 1998). A *Learning System* (used here with initial caps) is composed of the learner in communion with an eLearning system. In the context of future technologies, the learner can be considered an intelligent, complex adaptive system coevolving with its eLearning system; intelligent because the learner has an objective to learn and seeks to fulfill that objective, and complex because the mind is a highly complex system, learning is a complex process, and the eLearning system is moving into complexity as it identifies and adapts responses to learner patterns. Adaptive implies that the learner—and presumably the eLearning system—changes and adapts as learning occurs, and such changes typically impact the environment to some degree. Thus the learning process is autopoietic in the sense of Maturana and Varella's discussion of an organism's internal structural adaptation to its external environment (Maturana and Varela, 1987).

Why Energetic Learning is Important

Brain activity is the result of the absorption of energy by neurons as they fire. The human brain has about 100 billion neurons, with each neuron having up to 10,000 connections (Edelman, 1989; Hobson, 1994; Ratey, 2001; Begley, 2007). That's 10 to 100 times more connections in your brain than cells in your body. There's a neuronal network (patterns in the brain) for everything you have learned, every thought you have had, and every action you have taken (Zull, 2002).

The brain uses more energy as more neurons fire in the process of associating patterns, creating ideas (sequences of patterns) and learning in general. This can be measured. The development of sophisticated brain measurement instrumentation such as functional magnetic resonance imaging (fMR), electroencephalography (EEG) and transcranial magnetic stimulation (TMS) (Kurzweil, 2005; Amen, 2005) has facilitated an intense increase in neuroscience research and an understanding of how our brain functions. The fMR process provides indirect indicators of changes in blood flow (Andreason, 2005), that is, showing regions of the brain that are highly active through the direct measurement of the oxygen utilization. For example, we now know that in the minute you have spent reading this paragraph a number of synapses in your brain have changed, and the strength of some synapses and patterns of neural connections are different. We also know that the more you think about something (focus on it, reflect on it), the greater the physical change in your brain. We also know that the more connections new patterns (thoughts, etc.) have to historical memories of significance, the easier it will be to activate these thoughts in the future. The learning experience depends on associating patterns resulting from the "interactions between the physical constructs of neuronal networks inside the brain and the reality of the concrete world" (Zull, 2002, p. 209). The stronger the synaptic junctions in the pattern and the more the pattern is repeated, the easier it will be to recall in the future. This process has been explicated at length in earlier *VINE* articles (Bennet and Bennet, 2006; Bennet and Bennet, 2008),

Emotions play a large role in this process. In this context, emotions are considered signals or labels that are for the most part generated unconsciously. An emotional tag is linked to all information patterns coming into the brain. As Lipton explains,

> The evolution of the limbic system provided a unique mechanism that converted the chemical communication signals into sensations that could be experienced by all of the cells in the community. Our conscious mind experiences these *signals* as emotions. (Lipton, 2005, p. 131)

Thus, as part of our evolving learning system, memories and the emotional tags that gage the importance of those memories become part of an individual's everyday life. The *stronger the emotional tag*, the greater the strength of the connections (LeDoux, 2000) and the easier to recall. As Kluwe states, "Often we experience that emotionally arousing events result in better recollection of memories. It appears to us that we will not forget certain events in our life whenever they are accompanied by very pleasant or fearful emotions" (Kluwe, 2003, p. 51). This is true because *emotions have priority in our stream of consciousness*. Consciousness is comprised of a single, linear stream of thought patterns (Edelman and Tononi, 2000) and as such this mechanism of awareness can be filled with mundane facts or highly charged emotions. Through evolution (based on survival of the fittest) our brain has been wired such that the connections from the emotional systems to the cognitive systems are much stronger than the connections from the cognitive systems to the emotional systems. As LeDoux (1996) observes, "Emotions easily bump mundane events out of awareness, but non emotional events (like thoughts) do not so easily displace emotions from the mental spotlight" (p.19).

Not only can emotions preempt cognitive thought at the conscious level, but also since emotional processing can—and regularly does—take place outside of conscious awareness (LeDoux, 1996, p. 58), we may not be aware of what is driving our decisions and actions. Further, some studies have shown that our emotions are *more easily influenced* when we are not aware that the influence is occurring. The advertising industry regularly uses emotional cues (implicitly and explicitly) to persuade consumers to buy products (Packard, 1957). However, when understood, anything that can be used by others to manipulate us can also be used by us to manipulate ourselves. For example, by understanding that emotions are things that happen to us rather than things we order to occur, we can set up situations where external events provide stimuli to trigger desired emotions (LeDoux, 1996). We do this regularly when we go to the movies or visit an amusement park, or even when we consume alcohol or stimulate our palate with a gourmet meal.

Negative emotions appear to have a prominent presence in self-awareness and self-identity (Keenan, et al., 1999). This is because the right hemisphere of the brain (which is biased towards negative emotions that lead us to fight or distance ourselves from something or someone) develops in early childhood when we are developing our self-identity. Fear increases the chances of a child's survival; thus the emotions centered in the right hemisphere can override those centered in the left hemisphere (which with the expanded neocortex produces positive feelings related to humor, social affiliation and aesthetic responses) (Paradiso, et al., 1999; Wild, et al., 2003). The irony is that negative emotions do not generally promote learning. For example, it has been demonstrated that voluntary learning—choosing to learn—not only is marked by the absence of stress, but is also characterized by the presence of brain rhythms called theta waves which are present when you pay close attention to something (Begley, 2007, p. 68). In addition, the same fear that causes a fight or flight response can bring about negative long-term results for learning. As Byrnes observes,

> ... excessive levels of cortisol (a substance secreted by the adrenal glands during stress reactions) causes permanent damage to several regions of the brain, including the hippocampus (important for memory) and the locusceruleus (important for selective attention). Byrnes, 2001, p.181

Understanding and harnessing the power of emotion can improve an individual's ability to learn. Recall the old adage: *Follow your passion.* In the larger Learning System (the learner entangled with an eLearning system), this is the entry point to energetic learning. Passion is considered those desires, behaviors, and thoughts that suggest urges with considerable force (Frijda, 2000), specifically including Polanyi's assertion that positive passions affirm that something is precious, and that passion can be used as a determinant of what is of higher interest and great (Polanyi, 1958). A passion to learn or a deep passion related to the content of learning embeds strong emotional tags with what is being learned, directly impacting the *number* of synapse connections created and the *strength* of those connections. When positive emotions create this impact, learning becomes exciting and the memory of what is learned stays with us. Memory is further enhanced when learning includes meaning and understanding of the material.

Another aspect of energetic learning is the conscious intent to learn. In a study of information-processing receptors on nerve cell membranes, Pert discovered that emotions were not simply derived through a feedback of the body's environmental information, but that through self-consciousness the mind can use the brain to *generate* "molecules of emotion" and override the system (Pert, 1997). This self-conscious mind processing occurs in the prefrontal cortex (on the scale of evolution, the *newly evolved* organ that observes our behaviors and emotions) (Lipton, 133). This portion of the brain has access to most of the data stored in our long-term memory bank and is the executive part of the brain that solves problems, makes decisions and initiates actions (Goldberg, 2001). What this means is that our minds can *chose* to embed stronger emotional tags with specific incoming information. For example, this occurs when we engage new ideas and become excited about the potential offered by these new ideas for ourselves, our organizations, or our world. LeDoux believes that this struggle between thought and emotion may ultimately be resolved, by "a more harmonious integration of reason and passion in the brain, a development that will allow future humans to better know their true feelings and to use them more effectively in daily life" (LeDoux, 2002, p. 21).

Meanwhile, it is now clear that heredity cannot be fully blamed for an individual's inability to learn. Discoveries in neuroscience now indicate that DNA blueprints passed down through genes are not set in concrete at birth. As Lipton exclaims, "Genes are not destiny! Environmental influences, including nutrition, stress and emotions, can modify those genes, without changing their basic blueprint" (Lipton, 2005, p. 67). Not only can an individual change her own DNA, but an individual can affect the DNA that is passed on to future generations via the Double Helix (Reik and Walter, 2001; Surani, 2001).

eLearning Systems Themselves Contribute to Energetic Learning

The question is begged: How can eLearning best assist an individual in becoming an energetic learner? Clearly, there is no greater resource to information access than that offered through connected eLearning systems. The unlimited potential offered by an Internet-connected world may be the single most exciting development of the 20th Century, if not in the entire history of humanity; and Internet-savvy learners have a natural excitement as they sit at the keyboard connected to the world! The relevant question becomes, is a learner seeking information or knowledge? If it's an information dump that is needed, that is easily accommodated by a hook-up and providing the skills to search, select and retrieve information from the Internet. But if it's knowledge that is needed, then learning must be interactive and specifically tailored to each individual. Below we forward the value of eLearning systems—specifically in terms of their contribution to energetic learning—by first addressing the differences between information transfer and knowledge sharing, then providing three examples of eLearning in support of positive learning experiences followed by a short discussion of the semantic web concept in support of knowledge sharing.

The transfer of information is less sensitive to individual characteristics than the creation of knowledge. For the transfer of information, the learner simply has to memorize it, understanding its basic meaning, then apply it accordingly. Change the situation a bit and the incoming information may not solve your problem! This requires knowledge, the ability to take effective action in varied and uncertain situations. In order to create knowledge, the learner must not only understand the incoming information, but also mix it with his own internal experience to create the desired Knowledge (Informing) and Knowledge (Proceeding) within himself, that is, he must develop a deeper understanding of the information, insights into the situation, and anticipate the results of potential actions.

Knowledge *starts* with information, with an individual gathering the requisite Kn_I necessary to develop sufficient understanding of the meaning of that information in order to take effective action. An eLearning system moves from supporting information awareness to facilitating knowledge awareness when the focus of the system shifts from information storage, retrieval and transfer to creating and supporting collaborative environments for knowledge sharing. For example, knowledge (proceeding) can only be stored in a computer as it pertains to a specific, predesigned situation with a clear, logical, specific solution (a situation that in today's world may be rare). Such thinking would be more of a memory goal than that of developing or sharing knowledge.

Similarly, eLearning has been proven effective in skill training where specific information, causal relationships and repeated practice are required. Here, the learner must adapt to the needs of the skill and eLearning proves very cost effective. While this training may be done by video with student feedback, some content may require group training with an eLearning system, and perhaps a virtual instructor. Whichever the case, skill training is focused on information, manual operations and logical thinking with clear, predetermined results. This type of skill training may or may not engage the learner in energetic learning. However, if the desired performance requires not only skill but also a good understanding of the theory, nuances and uncertainties in the operation, the adaptivity and robustness of the eLearning system becomes significant to the learning experience. Now it is necessary for the eLearning system to adapt to the learners' needs in order to help them create the *knowledge* needed to deal with unexpected situations. As we might expect, physical and flight simulators, games, and even narratives—which can carry strong emotional tags—can be effectively employed in eLearning systems (Quinn, 2007). Progressive games offer the opportunity for long-term engagement. Wiig points out that the importance of a business simulation game lies in the learner's opportunity to participate actively over a period of time in an evolving situation. Thus learners are gathering embodied knowledge and internalizing how to assess situations, the implications of and results from the actions they take (Wiig, 2004; Bennet and Bennet, 2008).

This discussion has surfaced some clear advantages to eLearning in terms of supporting positive learning experiences. A first example is, with the advent of the Internet, the potential for immediate, just-in-time learning when it is needed and desired and a "no limits" experience in terms of availability and accessibility of information. A second example is, given the need for and advantages of collaboration, the opportunity to collaborate in world-wide learning experiences. Whether participating one-on-one or in a group collaborative situation, different viewpoints and perspectives can prove exciting and accelerate learning. There are more collaboration systems described as eLearning systems than there are authoring and service delivery systems, and most service delivery systems include collaboration and social networking tools. An assumed given is that participants are familiar with collaboration techniques such as appreciative inquiry, dialogue and critical thinking. Critical thinking is considered an essential collaborative tool because it encourages individuals to question their own beliefs and assumptions thereby opening the mind for other views and perspectives.

In a 2006 market research study by Ambient Insight, the U.S. market for real-time collaboration-based learning products and services was over $2.6 billion and growing at a five-year compound annual growth rate of 34.5 percent (Adkins, 2007). This trend has co-evolved with the expansion of communities of practice as work-sponsored learning structures. For example, in *The Story Behind Defense Acquisition University's Reinvention of Training*, Anderson and Hardy state,

Communities of Practice are one of our highest growth areas. We have almost twenty thousand registered members making almost fifty thousand contributions a month. We get over 2.5 million page visits per month and over 10 million page views. It's been an amazing addition to our university and an indispensable resource for the workforce. (Anderson, et al., 2008, p. 119)

In the formal U.S. education system, special collaboration software solutions are offered that provide safe collaborative environments for students from kindergarten to graduate levels. Examples are *Knowledge Forum* (making information accessible with multiple vantage points and multiple entry points) and *FirstClass* (supporting student publishing of blogs and podcasts). An example of open source collaborative learning software would be *Sakai*, which supports teaching and learning, both ad hoc and research collaboration. These environments engage youths in dynamic information exchange and personally-instigated social learning situations. In this setting, a popular eLearning software package is *Blackboard*, which includes a module for building online communities to improve information flow, and a module designed for learners to collect, present and reflect on their learning experiences, providing positive feedback to support sustained learning. During these collaboration efforts it is very important to recognize the distinction between information sharing and knowledge creation and sharing.

A third example is that eLearning can mitigate potential embarrassment in a classroom or human dialogue since it offers the opportunity for thinking before contributing. This may significantly enhance the learning process. However, note that "cold" language in an eLearning system may put-off a learner and create an uncomfortable atmosphere. Fortunately, this was a lesson learned early in the design of eLearning systems such that a "soft" compassionate language has been embedded within dialogue-driven programs and other interactive systems. For an individual who needs time to digest new ideas, eLearning provides a comfort zone. Long-term memory can be enhanced for any specific information through repetition. An eLearning system can precisely repeat over and over again what it is communicating; a human rarely can or will. Additionally, when designed to assess and provide quick feed-back from a positive perspective, an eLearning system can punctuate positive learning experiences and mitigate mis-learning. For example, if learning content is misunderstood the eLearning system can lead and support the learner to create their own improved understanding and *feel good about it*. A learner does not learn until she creates her own interpretation and understanding in terms of personal history, current beliefs and assumptions, and frame of reference. Therein lies the challenge to eLearning systems if they are to support the sharing of deep knowledge, that is, thorough understanding and good insights into the nature and operation of the situation.

Over the last few years there's been much discussion about development of a semantic web, the term used by Tim Berners-Lee to describe his vision of the Web as a universal medium for data, information and knowledge exchange. The semantic web would not only provide content, links and transactions between people and computers, but would finally make the dream of technology as an intelligent agent a reality, with machines talking to machines accomplishing the day-to-day mechanisms of trade (Berners-Lee and Fischetti, 1999). The term "semantic" is "of or related to meaning", specifically referring to language. While the level of "meaning" conveyed through the Semantic Web would vary substantially—dependent on the value and organization of information and the knowledge and skill sets of the individual using it—this "meaning" would be primarily associated with Knowledge (Informing). This is true because it would be impossible to convey all potential situations of applicability, and the information and its meaning would vary with each situation and its context. Clearly, the semantic web would facilitate dialogue and the sharing of information, and perhaps the sharing of knowledge as we learn more about the conversion of information to knowledge within the human mind. eLearning could become highly useful in knowledge sharing if it became context intelligent, semantically smart and dialogue proficient. There are very real challenges to address before this will be possible, not the least of which is semantic and syntactic interoperability. However, given enough time, this vision will undoubtedly become a reality.

Personalizing eLearning

A necessary step for effective eLearning systems is to support and assist the learner in creating Knowledge (Proceeding) through the recall and internal association of the right Knowledge (Informing) to determine the actions necessary to solve a problem. This requires the learner to practice solving problems to embed the processes of taking effective actions while reinforcing and demonstrating the effectiveness of their knowledge. Since a great deal of knowledge is tacit, and therefore cannot exist in a computer, eLearning systems cannot store or share all of the requisite Kn_I. However, using the information that is stored, an eLearning system can be designed to help learners surface their own tacit Kn_I related to specific areas of learning. This can be accomplished through a system that asks pertinent questions, evaluates answers according to specific situations and context, and "guides" learners towards becoming aware of and linking their own past experiences and knowledge to this new information.

In other words, there are no simple solutions. eLearning provides a platform for a *divergent learning approach* where there are multiple solutions and creative thinking is needed to solve problems. Divergent learning emphasizes concrete experience and reflective observation. It's greatest strength is the focus on imaginative ability and awareness of meaning and values (Kolb, 1984). For example, many personnel problems do not have a nice neat solution and require creative and situational-dependent thinking. The eLearning system participates in divergent learning by creating an active information environment where learners can both practice solving problems and creating their own problems to solve. When problems are posed with open-ended solutions, learners are pressed to think more about the subject, ask questions, and explore different *learning paths*. Glimpses of these approaches are beginning to appear in eLearning systems. While not yet student-driven, nor in the context of complex adaptive, an example of an open source program that helps teachers develop learning paths for students (and also uses the Wiki to write collaborative documents) is *About Claroline*. As the process of exploring different learning paths guides learners to discover insights on their own concerning the information, learning is enhanced. Introduced earlier, this is because the brain—as a knowledge seeking organism choosing its own path—maximizes its attention and focus, thereby creating emotions and releasing chemicals that enhance neuronal activity (Edelman and Tononi, 2000), positively reinforcing the brain's desire to learn.

Another significant aspect of personalizing learning is that information must be relevant, acceptable, understandable and motivational taking into account the individual's belief set, personal goals, cultural background, communication and learning styles, and prior knowledge, expertise and experience. From cognitive to emotional to embodied preferences, the uniqueness of the individual learner is a primary factor in learning. eLearning systems have the capacity to provide a spectrum of learning approaches to help accommodate these differences. Next-generation learning environments are being designed to support personalization, adaptivity and on-demand learning object generation (Brusilovsky, 2001). For example, this is the core focus in state-of-the-art Adaptive Hypermedia Systems (AHS) where a service-oriented architecture supports adaptive personalization through the use of individual services for the sourcing of learning content, the personalization of learning offerings, and the presentation of those offerings (Lawless, et al., 2008).

Instead of one learning model driving an eLearning system, there may be ten or twenty or thirty, each with a different perspective that would lead to the feel and semantics of the explanation. As the learner finds their own path, these patterns become entangled with the eLearning system, building a personalized program providing the capacity for the learner to navigate the path based on comfort, choice, and learning speed. Searching techniques in many software systems already include social tagging and ranking, and intuitive pattern development. User-defined learning paths are available in some full-spectrum and learning delivery systems such as *Desire2Learn*. In addition, a number of authoring programs such as *Lectora 2008* by Trivantis incorporate Variable Knowledge Objects to create branched learning scenarios. While eLearning systems cannot yet provide the full-spectrum transfer of embodied tacit knowledge that is possible over time between one human and another, materials can be communicated in totally different ways to provide the learner with a high probability of understanding the concepts presented. An advanced eLearning system could provide different varieties of the information content based on a spectrum such that the learner could resonate with the information provided by some part of the spectrum. One example is basing this spectrum on the MBTI, which describes 16 different preferences for accessing and processing information. Information around a specific topic could provide 16 different deliveries of information that resonate with the corresponding MBTI types (Kroeger, O. and Thuesen, J.M., 1988; Myers, I.B. with Myers, P.B., 1993; Hirsh, S.K. and Kummerow, J., 1997; Kummerow, J.M., et al., 1997). Another presentation form could be based on the Kolb learning styles inventory (Kolb, 1984). But this still doesn't' address the fundamental issues of optimizing learning capacity through understanding the specific nature and context of a situation, or the learner's history and frame of reference. At least not yet.

For many years there were attempts to build computers that can think like humans. It is not simply the large number of connections (synapses) in the human brain that make this difficult, and it is not *what* the human brain does but understanding *how* it does it—that step portrayed in a myriad of cartoons that says "then a miracle occurs"—that challenges the designer's intellect. Building on the early connection machines made by Thinking Machines, Inc. (Hillis, 1987), at the turn of the 21st century Brown University set out to build a brain-like computer, what was called the Ersatz Brain Project. While only focusing on a microcosm of the brain, when the project was over the team had recognized that by requiring software to use brain-like constraints new ways to tackle old problems emerged (Anderson and Allopenna). Further, they realized that an important application of such a machine would be the realization of a large network where individual nodes having complex internal structures would provide flexibility and associative capabilities beyond semantic networks. The understanding was beginning to be voiced that as we design machines to mimic our minds we need to make sure that those machines are equipped with sufficient diversity. They need a similar diversity to that which distinguishes humans from most other animals and from machines built in the past, "stemming from what we each have made of ourselves: a colossal collection of different ways to deal with different situations and predicaments" (Minsky, 2006, p. 6).

Moving beyond Artificial Intelligence approaches to exploration of this technology to aid learning and decision-making, in 2005 cognitive science and technology became a core research focus for Sandia National Laboratories. For Sandia, cognitive systems include technologies that utilize computational models of human cognitive processes or knowledge of specific experts or other individuals (Sandia, 2007). These systems accurately infer user intent, remember experiences and provide simulated experts to help users analyze situations and make decisions. Through modeling a virtual "you" and simulating thinking patterns, individual strengths can be reinforced and weaknesses mitigated. Imagine this as the basis for a learning system, a human-technology partnering that is already beginning to happen today. This is clearly not the AI of the past. As described by Chris Forsythe, intent is modeled to a specific individual; knowledge is associative with emphasis on pattern recognition not just rule-based representations and logic; and this is a dynamic complex system that may easily adapt to changing circumstances (Forsythe, 2003).

Emphasizing the significance of emotions in learning, out of MIT in 1997 emerged the field of affective computing. Affective computing is described as computing that relates to, arises from or deliberately influences emotions (Picard, 1997). Embedding the ability to recognize emotions into machines was driven by Picard's belief that putting emotions in machines would not only make them more human (thereby improving human-computer communication), but could lead to a more human decision-making process supporting decision-makers and learners. Further, "When we succeed, a feeling of pride might encourage us to keep on going and push ourselves even harder to reach even greater goals" (Neji and Ben Ammar, 2007). Since emotions are contagious, it is this contagious nature that Neiji and Ben Ammar felt was potentially transferable and beneficial to the virtual world. Recognizing that the use of emotions to complement and indeed facilitate communication in collaborative virtual environments had been vastly under-explored, they developed a collaborative affective eLearning framework aimed at reintroducing emotional and social context to distance learning while offering a stimulating and integrated framework for affective conversation and collaboration. In essence, they were proposing an emotional framework for an intelligent emotional system.

Final Thoughts

Through the process of evolution the human mind was designed to learn for itself. Cave men learned via a watching and doing loop. It wasn't until the last few hundred years that the education process took on the rigidness of industrial age efficiency, herding children together in school rooms in order to turn out large numbers of individuals labeled as "educated". This process, of course, is counter to learning in terms of evolution of the species. Neither man nor machine can force an individual to remember, understand, or feel good about learning, so necessary for living and surviving in an uncertain and complex world. Learning is a very private affair, dependent upon the needs, feelings, history and expectations of the self-organizing system made up of the mind, the brain, the body, the spirit, the conscious self, and—in our example, and in our world—the eLearning system.

Focusing on the value of energetic learning, with technology comes a natural excitement in terms of connectivity to the world, as well as its capability to support self-driven, experiential learning which is part of our evolutionary heritage. This excitement can help accelerate our journey as we continue to discover our full potential as learners, consciously engaging and embedding emotional tags and fully exploiting the beauty and complexity of our mind-brain-body-spirit combination. As technology moves into a closer partnering relationship with the human mind, anything is possible.

Appendix A References

Adkins, S. S. (2007), "Data File: Real-Time Collaboration", *Learning Circuits*, downloaded at http:///www.learningcircuits.org/2007/0207adkins.htm (February 2008).

Amen, Daniel G. (2005), *Making a Good Brain Great*, Harmony Books, New York, NY.

Anderson, J. A. and Allopenna, P, "A brain-like computer for cognitive applications: The Ersatz Brain Project", downloaded from www.cog.brown.edu/Research/ErsatzBrainGroup/index.html (February, 2008).

Anderson, F. J., Hardy, C. R. and Leeson, J. (2008), *Leading a Learning Revolution: The Story Behind Defense Acquisition University's Reinvention of Training*, Pfeiffer, San Francisco, CA.

Andreasen, N. C. (2005),*The Creating Brain: The Neuroscience of Genius*, Dana Press, New York, NY.

Begley, S. (2007), *Train Your Mind Change Your Brain: How a New Science Reveals Our Extraordinary Potential to Transform Ourselves*, Ballantine Books, New York, NY.

Bennet, A. and Bennet, D. (2008), "Engaging tacit knowledge in support of organizational learning", in *VINE: The Journal of Information and Knowledge Management Systems*, Vol. 40. No. 1, 2008.

Bennet, A. and Bennet, D. (2007), "CONTEXT: The shared knowledge enigma", in *VINE, The Journal of Information and Knowledge Management Systems,* Vol 37, No. 1, pp. 27-40.

Bennet, A. and Bennet, D. (2006), "Learning as associative patterning", in *VINE: The Journal of Information and Knowledge Management Systems*, Vol. 36. No. 4, pp. 371-376.

Bennet, A. and Bennet, D. (2004),*Organizational Survival in the New World: The Intelligent Complex Adaptive System*, Elsevier, Boston, MA.

Berners-Lee, T. and Fischetti, M. (1999), *Weaving the Web: The Original Design and Ultimate Destiny of the World Wide Web by Its Inventor*, HarperCollins, New York, NY.

Brusilovsky, P. (2001), "Adaptive hypermedia" in *User Modelling and User-Adapted Interaction*, 87-110, March, Springer.

Byrnes, J. P. (2001),*Minds, Brains, and Learning: Understanding the Psychological and Educational Relevance of Neuroscientific Research*, The Guilford Press, New York, NY.

Edelman, G. M. (1989),*The Remembered Present: A Biological Theory of Consciousness*, Basic Books, New York, NY.

Edelman, G. M. and Tononi, G. (2000), *A Universe of Consciousness: How Matter Becomes Imagination*, Basic Books, New York, NY.

Forsythe, C. (2003), "Human-machine interface possibilities: What if the machine is a human-like cognitive entity?" downloaded from www.sandia.gov/cog.systems/Index.html (February, 2008).

Frijda, N. H. (2000), The psychologists' point of view" in Lewis, M. and Haviland-Jones, J.M. (Eds.), *Handbook of Emotions*, The Guilford Press, New York, NY.

Goldberg, E. (2001),*The Executive Brain: Frontal Lobes and the Civilized Mind*, Oxford University Press, New York, NY.

Hillis, W.D. (1987),*The Connection Machine*, MIT Press, Cambridge, MA.

Hirsh, S.K. and Kummerow, J. (1997), *Life Types*, Warner Books, New York, NY.

Hobson, J. A. (1999), *Consciousness*, Scientific American Library, New York, NY.

Johnson, S. and Taylor, K. (Eds.) (2006),*The Neuroscience of Adult Learning*, Jossey-Bass, San Francisco, CA.

Keenan, J. P., McCutcheon, B., Freund, S., Gallup, G. G., Jr., Sanders, G. and Pascual-Leone, A. (1999), "Left hand advantage in self-face recognition task" in *Neuropsychologia*, 37, 1421-1425.

Kluwe, Rainer H., Luer, Gerd, and Rosler, Frank (Eds.) (2003), *Principles of Learning and Memory*, Birkhauser Verlag, Basel, Switzerland.

Kolb, D.A. (1984), *Experiential Learning: Experience as the Source of Learning and Development*, Prentice Hall, Englewood Cliffs, NJ.

Kroeger, O. and Thuesen, J.M. (1988), *Type Talk*, Dell Publishing, New York, NY.

Kummerow, J.M., Barger, N.J. and Kirby, L.K. (1997), *Work Types*, Warner Book, New York, NY.

Kurzweil, R. (2005), *The Singularity is Near: When Humans Transcend Biology*, Viking Penguin, New York, NY.

Lawless, S., Wade, V., and Conlan, O., "Dynamic contextual eLearning—Dynamic content discovery, capture and learning object generation from open corpus sources", Trinity College, Dublin, Ireland, downloadable at http://kdeg.cs.tcd.ie

LeDoux, J. (1996),*The Emotional Brain: The Mysterious Underpinnings of Emotional Life*, Touchstone, New York, NY.

Lipton, B. (2005),*The Biology of Belief: Unleashing the Power of Consciousness, Matter and Miracles*, Elite Books, Santa Rosa, CA.

Maturana, H.R. and Varela, F. J. (1987),*The Tree of Knowledge: The Biological Roots of Human Understanding*, Shambhala, Boston, MA.

Minsky, M. (2006), *The Emotion Machine: Commonsense Thinking, Artificial Intelligence, and the Future of the Human Mind*, Simon and Schuser, New York, NY.

Myers, I.B. with Myers, P.B. (1993), *Gifts Differing: Understanding Personality Type*, CPP Books, Palo Alto, CA.

Neji, M. and Ben Ammar, M. (2007), "Emotional eLearning system", presentation to the Fourth International Conference on eLearning for Knowledge-Based Society, November 18-19, Bangkok, Thailand.

Netday and Blackboard (2006), "Learning in the 21st Century: A National Report of Online Learning", downloaded from http://www.blackboard.com/inpractice/K12/onlinelearningreport (February, 2008).

Packard, V. (1957), *The Hidden Pesuaders*, D. M. McKay, New York, NY.

Paradiso, S., Johnson, D.L., Andreasen, N.C., O'Leary, D.S., Watkins, G.L., Ponto, L.L.B., et al. (1999), "Cerebral blood flow changes associated with attribution of emotional valence to pleasant, unpleasant, and neutral visual stimuli in a PET study of normal subjects", in *American Journal of Psychiatry*, 156, 1618-1629.

Pert, C. (1997), *Molecules of Emotion: The Science Behind Mind-Body Medicine*, Scribner, New York, NY.

Picard, R. W. (1997), *Affective Computing*, MIT Press, Cambridge, MA.

Polanyi, M. (1958), *Personal Knowledge: Towards a Post-Critical Philosophy*, The University of Chicago Press, Chicago, IL.

Quinn, C. (2007), "Computer-based simulations: Principles of engagement", in Siberman, Mel (Ed.), *The Handbook of Experiential Learning*, John Wiley & Sons, Inc., San Francisco, CA.

Ratey, J.J. (2001), *A User's Guide to the Brain: Perception, Attention, and the Four Theaters of the Brain*, Pantheon Books, New York, NY.

Reik, W. and Walter, J. (2001), "Genomic imprinting: Parental influence on the genome", in *Nature Reviews Genetics* 2: 21+.

Ryle, G. (1949), *The Concept of Mind*, Hutchinson, London, England.

Salomon, G., Perkins, D.N. and Globerson, T. (1991), "Partners in cognition: Extending human intelligence with intelligent technologies", in *Educational Researcher*, 20.

Sandia National Laboratories (2007), "Cognitive Science and technology program becomes Sandia initiative", news release, August 8.

Stonier, T. (1997), *Information and Meaning: An Evolutionary Perspective*, Springer, New York, NY.

Stonier, T. (1992), *Beyond Information: The Natural History of Intelligence*, Springer-Verlag, New York, NY.

Surani, M. A. (2001), "Reprogramming of genome function through epigenetic inheritance", in *Nature* 414: 122+.

Wiig, K. (2004), *People-Focused Knowledge Management: How Effective Decision Making Leads to Corporate Success*, Elsevier Butterworth Heinemann, New York, NY

Wikipedia (2008). "Energetics", downloaded from http://en.wikipedia.org/wiki/Energetics (March, 2008).

Wild, B., Rodden, F.A., Grodd, W. and Ruch, W. (2003), "Neural correlates of laughter and humor", in *Brain*, 126, 2121-2138.

Zull, J.E. (2002), *The Art of Changing the Brain: Enriching the Practice of Teaching by Exploring the Biology of Learning*, Stylus, Sterling.

Appendix B

The Human Knowledge System: Music and Brain Coherence

Alex Bennet, Ph.D., and David Bennet, Ph.D.

Abstract

Purpose—This paper explores the relationship between music and learning in the mind/brain.

Design/methodology/approach—Taking a consilience approach, this paper briefly introduces how music affects the mind/brain, then moves through several historical highlights of our emergent understanding of the role of music in learning—for example, the much-misunderstood Mozart effect. Then the role of music in learning is explored from a neuroscience perspective, with specific focus on its potential to achieve brain coherence. Finally, using a specific example of sound technology focused on achieving hemispheric synchronization, research findings, anecdotes, and experiential interactions are integrated to touch on the potential offered by this new understanding.

Findings—Listening to music regularly (along with replaying tunes in our brains) clearly helps our neurons stay active and alive and our synapses intact. Listening to the right music does appear to facilitate learning, and participating more fully in music making appears to provide additional cerebral advantages. Further, some music supports hemispheric synchronization, offering the opportunity to achieve brain coherence and significantly improve learning.

Keywords—Music, Learning, Brain Coherence, Hemispheric Synchronization, the Mozart effect, Transfer Effects

Introduction

When Charles Darwin wrote his Autobiography in 1887, he was moved to say,

If I had to live my life again I would have made a rule to read some poetry and listen to some music at least once a week; for perhaps the parts of my brain now atrophied could thus have been kept active through use (Amen 2005, 158).

Today, there's no doubt that the brain atrophies through disuse, that is, neurons die and synapses wither when they are not used (Zull 2002), but would listening to music once a week have kept more of those neurons and synapses active and alive? And if so, what if we participated more fully in music making? How could we maximize our learning?

In this paper we briefly introduce how music affects the mind/brain, then move through several historical highlights of our emergent understanding of the role of music in learning—for example, the much-misunderstood Mozart effect. Then we explore the role of music in learning from a neuroscience perspective, with specific focus on its potential to achieve brain coherence. Finally, using a specific example of sound technology focused on achieving hemispheric synchronization, we integrate research findings, anecdotes, and experiential interactions to touch on the potential offered by this new understanding.

The approach of this exploration through the literature—peppered with anecdotes and experience—is one of consilience; specifically, the integrating of knowledge from a variety of fields to discover a common groundwork of explanation (Wilson 1991). This paper considers the findings of, among others, psychologists, physicists, neuroscientists, musicians, educators, biologists, engineers, and medical doctors.

Brain coherence is considered the orderly and harmonious connectedness between the two hemispheres of the brain—in other words, when the two hemispheres of the brain are synchronized, thus the term hemispheric synchronization. Borrowing from physics, when the brain is in a coherent state, systems are performing optimally and virtually no energy is wasted.[1] This, then, would be considered an optimal state for learning.

While specialization and selection occur in various parts of the brain, they do not occur independently (Levy 1985). As will be demonstrated, one of the "jobs" of music in the process of evolution and growth is to increase the interconnections between the two hemispheres of the brain. We begin.

How Music Affects the Mind/Brain

Music and the human mind have a unique relationship that is not yet fully understood. As Hodges forwards,

By studying the effects of music, neuroscientists are able to discover things about the brain that they cannot know through other cognitive processes. Likewise, through music we are able to discover, share, express, and know about aspects of the human experience that we cannot know through other means. Musical insights into the human condition are uniquely powerful experiences that cannot be replaced by any other form of experience (Hodges 2000, 21).

While the effect of music on the critical aspects of learning, attention, and memory may be a relatively new area of focused research, the human brain may very well be hardwired for music. As Weinberger, a neuroscientist at the University of California at Irvine, says, "An increasing number of findings support the theory that the brain is specialized for the building blocks of music" (Weinberger 1995, 6). Wilson, a biologist, goes even farther as he states that "all of us have a biologic guarantee of musicianship, the capacity to respond to and participate in the music of our environment" (cited in Hodges 2000, 18).

Sousa (2006) forwards that there are four proofs that support the biological basis for music: (1) it is universal (past–present, all cultures) (Swain 1997); (2) it reveals itself early in life (infants three months old can learn and remember to move an overhead crib mobile when a song is played [Fagan et al. 1997], and within a few months can recognize melodies and tones [Weinberger 2004; Hannon and Johnson 2005]); (3) it should exist in other animals besides humans (monkeys can form musical abstractions) (Sousa 2006); and (4) we might expect the brain to have specialized areas for music.

Exactly where this hardwiring might be located would be difficult to say. For example, even though there is an area in adults identified as the auditory cortex, visual information goes into the auditory cortex, just as auditory information goes into the visual cortex. That is why certain types of music can stimulate memory recall and visual imagery (Nakamura et al. 1999). Further, the auditory cortex is not inherently different from the visual cortex. Thus, "Brain specialization is not a function of anatomy or dictated by genes. It is a result of experience" (Begley 2007, 108). This process of specialization through experience begins shortly after the time of conception—selecting and connecting. Many of the interconnections remain into adulthood, or perhaps throughout life. While these connections are not exercised in most adults—they are more like back-road connections—when the brain is deprived of one sense (for example, hearing or seeing), a radical reorganization occurs in the cortex, and connections that heretofore lay dormant are used to expand the remaining senses (Begley 2007).

In the early phases of neuronal growth (during the first few months of life), there is an explosion of synapses in preparation for learning (Edelman 1992). Yet beginning around the age of eight months through sixteen months, tens of billions of synapses in the auditory and visual cortices are lost (Zull 2002). Chugani (1998) says that this explosion is concurrent with synaptic death, with experiences determining which synapses live or die. As Zull explains, before eight months of age synapses are being formed faster than they are being lost. Then things shift, and we begin to lose more synapses than we create (Zull 2002). The brain is sculpting itself through interaction with its environment, with the reactions of the brain determining its own architecture.

This process of selection continues as the rest of life is played out. This is the process of learning, selecting, connecting, and changing our neuronal patterns (Edelman 1992; Zull 2002). Music plays a core role in this process. Jensen contends that "music can actually prime the brain's neural pathways" (2000b, 246).

The brain has the capacity to structurally change throughout life. As Begley describes, "The actions we take can literally expand or contract different regions of the brain, pour more juice into quiet circuits and damp down activity in buzzing ones" (Begley 2007, 8). During this process of plasticity, the brain is expanding areas for functions used more frequently and shrinking areas devoted to activities that are rarely performed.

Further, in the late 1990s neuroscientific researchers discovered that the structure of the brain can change as a result of the thoughts we have. As Dobbs explains, the neurons that are scattered throughout key parts of the brain "fire not only as we perform a certain action, but also when we watch someone else perform that action" (Dobbs 2007, 22). These are mirror neurons, a form of mimicry that bypasses cognition, transferring actions, behaviors, and most likely other cultural norms quickly and efficiently. Thus when we see something being enacted, our mind creates the same patterns that we would use to enact that "something" ourselves. Because people have stored representations of songs and sounds in their long-term memory, music can be imagined. When a tune is moving through your mind it is activating the same cells as if you were hearing it from the outside world. Further, as we have noted, when you are internally imagining a tune, the visual cortex is also stimulated such that visual patterns are occurring as well (Sousa 2006).

Not all of these findings were known when music and acoustic pioneer Alfred Tomatis (1983) forwarded the analogy that sound provided an electrical charge to energize the brain. He described cells in the cortex of the brain as acting like small batteries, generating the electricity viewed in an EEG printout. What he discovered that was amazing was that these batteries were not charged by the metabolism, but rather through sound from an external source. With the discovery of mirror neurons, this would mean that imagining tunes is also providing a charge. These early Tomatis studies found that sound impacted posture, energy flow, attitude, and muscle tone, and that the greatest impact was in the 8000-hertz frequency range (Tomatis 1983; Jensen 2000b). Other research took this further, suggesting that low-frequency tones caused a discharge of mental and physical energy and certain higher tones powered up the brain (Clynes 1982; Zatorre 1997).

Researcher Frances Rauscher (1997) contends that music appreciation and abstract reasoning have the same neural firing patterns; however, this was observed in research that occurred several years after her earlier studies introducing the controversial Mozart effect and setting in motion a growing interest in the relationship of music and learning.

The Mozart Effect

The Mozart effect emerged in 1993 with a brief paper published in Nature by Frances Rauscher, Gordon Shaw, and Katherine Ky. To discover whether a brief exposure to certain music increased cognitive ability, the researchers divided thirty-six college students into three groups and used standard intelligence subtests to measure spatial/temporal reasoning.

Spatial/temporal reasoning is considered "the ability to form mental images from physical objects, or to see patterns in time and space" (Sousa 2006, 224). During the subtests one group worked in silence, one group listened to a tape of relaxation instructions, and the third group listened to a Mozart piano sonata (specifically, Mozart's Sonata for Two Pianos in D Major). There were significantly higher results in the Mozart group, although the effect was brief, lasting only ten to fifteen minutes (Rauscher, Shaw, and Ky 1993).

The Mozart effect quickly became a meme, taking on a life of its own completely out of the context of the findings. Perhaps this was because it was the first study relating music and spatial reasoning, suggesting that listening to music actually increased brain performance. There ensued high media coverage with the emphasis placed on the most sensational findings. The details of the study, however—specifically, that these findings were limited to spatial reasoning, not general intelligence, and that the effect was short-lived (ten to fifteen minutes)—were not part of the meme.

In 1994, Rauscher, Shaw, and Ky performed a follow-on study that was more extensive than the first. This five-day study involved seventy-nine college students who were pretested for their level of spatial/temporal reasoning prior to three listening experiences and then post-tested. While it was found that all students benefited (again, for a short period of time), the greatest benefits accrued to those students who had tested the lowest on spatial/temporal reasoning at the beginning of the experiment (Rauscher, Shaw, and Ky 1995).

By now, other groups were exploring the Mozart effect. The results were similar to the earlier results, again, for a short period of time (Rideout and Laubach 1996; Rideout and Taylor 1997; Rideout, Dougherty, and Wernert 1998; Wilson and Brown 1997). A series of similar studies with slightly different approaches, however, demonstrated no relevant differences between the group listening to Mozart and the control group (Steele, Brown, and Stoecker 1999a, 1999b; Chabris 1999). Still another study began with the premise that the complex melodic variations in Mozart's sonata provided greater stimulation to the prefrontal cortex than simpler music. When this theory was tested it was discovered that the Mozart sonata activated the auditory as well as the prefrontal cortex in all of the subjects, thus suggesting a neurological basis for the Mozart effect (Muftuler et al. 1999). Other specific case results were emerging. For example, Johnson et al. (1998) reported improvement in spatial-temporal reasoning in an Alzheimer's patient; and Hughes, Fino, and Melyn (1999) reported that a Mozart sonata reduced brain seizures.

As the exaggerated sensation of the initial finding began to sink into disillusionment, other researchers were building more understanding of the effect. For example, it was determined that while listening to Mozart before testing might improve spatial/temporal reasoning, listening to Mozart during testing could cause neural competition through interference with the brain's neural firing patterns (Felix 1993). Studies expanded to include other musical pieces. Researchers at the University of Texas Imaging Center in San Antonio discovered that "other subsets of music actually helped the experimental subjects do far better than did listening to Mozart" (Jensen 2000b, 247). Thus it was determined that the effect was not caused by the specific music of Mozart as much as the rhythms, tones, or patterns of Mozart's music that enhanced learning (Jensen 2000b). This is consistent with earlier work by researcher King (1991), who suggested that there is no statistically significant difference between New Age music and Baroque music in the effectiveness of inducing alpha states for learning (approximately 8–13 Hz), that is, they both enhance learning. Georgi Lozanov, a pioneer of accelerated learning, however, had said that classical and romantic music (circa 1750–1825 and 1820–1900, respectively) provided a better background for introducing new information (Lozanov 1991), and Clynes (1982) had recognized a greater consistency in body pulse response to classical music than rock music, which means that the response to classical music was more predictable.

Considering the exaggerated early claims, publicized without context and based on highly situation-dependent and context-sensitive studies, and the differences in findings among various research groups, it is easy to understand why the Mozart effect has proved so controversial. Note that the Mozart Effect emerged from studies involving adults (not children) and that it involved short periods of listening to specific music and doing specific subtasks to measure spatial/temporal reasoning. In these studies, effects from long-term listening were not studied or assessed, nor was the richer long-term involvement of learning and playing music. This brings us to a discussion of transfer effects.

Transfer Effects

The question of if and how music improves the mind is often couched as a question of transfer effects. This refers to the transfer of learning that occurs when improvement of one cognitive ability or motor skill is facilitated by prior learning or practice in another area (Weinberger 1999). For example, riding a bike, often used to represent embodied tacit knowledge (Bennet and Bennet 2008), is a motor skill (in descriptive terms, learning to maintain balance while moving forward) that can facilitate learning to skate or ski.

In cognitive and brain sciences the transfer of learning is a fundamental issue. While it has been argued that simply using a brain region for one activity does not necessarily increase competence in other skills or activities based in the same region (Coch, Fischer, and Dawson 2007), with our recent understanding of the power of thought patterns, one discipline is not completely independent of another (Hetland 2000). For example, a melody can act as a vehicle for a powerful communication transfer at both the conscious and nonconscious levels (Jensen 2000b). Thus, "Music acts as a premium signal carrier, whose rhythms, patterns, contrasts, and varying tonalities encode any new information" (Webb and Webb 1990). By "encode" is meant to facilitate remembering. An example is the "Alphabet Song" sung to the tune of "Twinkle, Twinkle Little Star."

There are different spectral types of real sounds coming from a myriad of sources. Periodic sounds that give a strong sense of pitch are harmonic (sung vowels, trumpets, flutes); those that have a weak or ambiguous sense of pitch are inharmonic (bells, gongs, some drums); and sound that has a sense of high or low but no clear sense of pitch is noise (consonants, some percussion instruments, and initial attacks of both harmonic and inharmonic sounds) (Soundlab 2005). Specific sounds we hear may include different spectral types; music often includes all three. For example, when hearing a church soloist, the noise of a strong consonant is followed by a sung vowel (harmonic). It is also noteworthy that the same part of the brain that hears pitch (the temporal lobe) is also involved in understanding speech (Amen 2005). Thus, specific combinations of sound may carry specific meaning by triggering memories or feelings whether or not they have words connected to them.

Research findings indicate that music actually increases certain brain functions that improve other cognitive tasks. Perhaps one of the most stunning results in the literature was achieved by a professional musician in North Carolina who was music director of the Winston-Salem Piedmont Triad Symphony Orchestra. The music director arranged for a woodwind quintet to play two or three half-hour programs per week at a local elementary school for three years: the first year playing for all first graders; the second year playing for all first and second graders; and the third year playing for all first, second, and third graders. Note that 70 percent of the students at the elementary school received free or reduced-price lunches. Prior to the study, first through fifth graders had an average composite IQ score of 92, and more than 60 percent of third graders tested below their grade level. Three years into the program, testing of the third graders exposed to the quintet music for three years showed remarkable differences, with 85 percent of this group testing above grade level for reading and 89 percent testing above grade level for math (Campbell 2000).

The limbic system and subcortical region of the brain—the part of the brain involved in long-term memory—are engaged in musical and emotional responses. When information is tied to music, therefore, it has a better chance of being encoded in long-term memory (Jensen 2000b). Context-dependent memory connected to music is not a new idea. In a study at Texas A&M University examining the role of background instrumental music in memory, music turned out to be an important contextual element. Subjects had the best recall when music was played during learning and that same music was played during recall (Godden and Baddeley 1975). This was confirmed in a 1993 study monitoring cortical and verbal responses to harmonic and melodic intervals in adults knowledgeable in music. The results showed consistent brain responses to intervals, whether isolated harmonic intervals, pairs of melodic intervals, or pairs of harmonic intervals. These results indicated that intervals may be viewed as meaningful words (Cohen et al. 1993).

It has also been found that background music enhances the efficiency of individuals who work with their hands. For example, in a study of surgeons it was found that background music increased their alertness and concentration (Restak 2003). The music that surgeons said worked best was not "easy-listening"; rather, that music was (in order of preference): Vivaldi's Four Seasons, Beethoven's Violin Concerto Op. 61, Bach's Brandenburg concertos, and Wagner's "Ride of the Valkyries." The use of background music during surgery did not cause interference and competition, since music and skilled manual activities activate different parts of the brain (Restak 2003). This, of course, is similar to the use of background music in the classroom or in places of work.

Dowling, a music researcher, believes that music learning affects other learning for different reasons. Building on the concepts of declarative memory and procedural memory, he says that music combines mind and body processes into one experience. For example, by integrating mental activities and sensory-motor experiences (like moving, singing, or participating rhythmically in the acquisition of new information, and for our doctors in the example above, their hand movements) learning occurs "on a much more sophisticated and profound level" (Campbell 2000, 173). Conversely, it has also been found that stimulating music can serve as a distraction and interfere with cognitive performance (Hallam 2002). Thus, much as determined in the early Mozart studies, different types of music produce different effects in different people in regard to learning.

The Right and Left Hemispheres of the Brain

The human brain is divided into two hemispheres, simply referred to as the right and left hemispheres. It was previously believed that the right hemisphere was the seat of music, but today we know that both sides of the brain are used to listen to music (Amen 2005). Music engages the whole brain (Jensen 2000b). For example, as sound enters the ears it goes to the auditory cortex in the temporal lobes. The temporal lobe in the nondominant hemisphere (generally the right hemisphere) hears pitch, melody, harmony, and beat and (recognizing long-term patterns) puts this together as a whole piece. The temporal lobe in the dominant hemisphere (generally the left hemisphere) is better at analyzing the incoming sound and hearing the short-term signatures of music, that is, lyrics and changes in rhythm (pacing), frequency, intensity, and harmonies (Amen 2005; Jensen 2000b; Weinberger 1995). The frontal lobe associates the sound with thought and stimulates emotions (in the limbic system) and past experiences (from memory scattered all over the brain) (Sousa 2006), and the cerebellum becomes involved in measuring the beats (spatial aspects) (Jensen 2000b). For example, while a non-musician would process music primarily in the right hemisphere (with potential strong contributions from the limbic system stimulated by the frontal lobe), a musician who was analyzing the content of a musical form would tend to hear music with his left hemisphere (Amen 2005) with a heavy dose of the cerebellum thrown in (Jensen 2000b).

Using PET scans, Eric Jensen, an educator known for his translation of neuroscience, has identified the various brain regions activated by different aspects of music. For example, rhythm activates Broca's area as well as the cerebellum; melody activates both hemispheres (with a specific recognized melody activating the right hemisphere); harmony activates the left hemisphere more than the right as well as the inferior temporal cortex; pitch activates the left back of the brain and may also activate the right auditory cortex; and timbre activates the right hemisphere (Jensen 2000b).

Further, activation of various parts of the brain is highly dependent on which senses are involved: aural (hearing music), sight (reading music), or touch (playing music). Other events, such as hearing a story about the Mozart effect, recalling a Rolling Stones concert, or having an emotional response to certain music, are processed differently in the brain (Jensen 2002). In other words, the experience and thought related to music is spatially diffused throughout the brain. While there are many studies on the connections between music and emotion and between emotion and learning, these are outside the focus of this paper.

As Robert Zatorre, a neuropsychologist at the Montreal Neurological Institute forwards, there is little doubt that music engages the entire brain. Further, as music has shifted over the last hundred years from Baroque or classical (stimulating our nondominant hemisphere) to more avant-garde styles (stimulating our dominant hemisphere), it has engaged the brain even more fully (Zatorre 1997).

Impact of Musical Instruction

Substantiating the long-held "knowing" that music is beneficial to human beings Hodges outlines five basic premises that establish a link between the human brain and the ability to learn. The first two confirm our earlier discussion of the brain as being hardwired for—or at least having a proclivity for—music. The latter three are pertinent to our forthcoming discussion of the impact of musical instruction on the learning mind/brain. As Hodges forwards (with some paraphrasing): (1) the human brain has the ability to respond to and participate in music; (2) the musical brain operates at birth and persists throughout life; (3) early and ongoing musical training affects the organization of the musical brain; (4) the musical brain consists of extensive neural systems involving widely distributed, but locally specialized, regions of the brain; and (5) the musical brain is highly resilient (Hodges 2000, 18).

There are hundreds of studies that confirm that creating music and playing music, especially when started at an early age, provide many more cerebral advantages than listening to music. In a study involving ninety boys between the ages of six and fifteen, it was discovered that musically trained students had better verbal memory (but showed no differences in visual memory). Thus musical training appeared to improve the ability of the Broca's and Wernicke's areas to handle verbal learning. Further, the memory benefits appeared long lasting. When students who dropped out of music training were tested a year later, it was found that they had retained the verbal memory advantage gained while in music training (Ho, Cheung, and Chan 2003).

Music and mathematics are closely related in brain activity (Abeles and Sanders 2005; Catterall, Chapleau, and Iwanga 1999; Graziano, Peterson, and Shaw 1999; Kay 2000; Schmithhorst and Holland 2004; Vaughn 2000). Mathematical concepts basic to music include patterns, counting, geometry, rations and proportions, equivalent fractions, and sequences (Sousa 2006). For example, musicians learn to recognize patterns of chords, notes, and key changes to create and vary melodies, and by inverting those patterns they create counterpoint, forming different kinds of harmonies. As further examples, musical beats and rests are counted, instrument finger positions form geometrical shapes, reading music requires an understanding of ratios and proportions (duration and relativity of notes), and a musical interval (sequence) is the difference between two frequencies (known as the beat frequency) (Sousa 2006).

In the brain, music is stored in a pitch-invariant form, that is, the important relationships (patterns) in the song are stored, not the actual notes. This can be demonstrated by an individual's ability to recognize a melody regardless of the key in which it is played (with different notes being played than those stored in memory). As Hawkins and Blakeslee detail,

> This means that each rendition of the "same" melody in a new key is actually an entirely different sequence of notes! Each rendition stimulates an entirely different set of locations on your cochlea, causing an entirely different set of spatial-temporal patterns to stream up into your auditory cortex ... and yet you perceive the same melody in each case (Hawkins and Blakeslee 2004, 80–81).

Unless you have perfect pitch, it is difficult to differentiate the two different keys. This means that—similar to other thought patterns—the natural approach to music storage, recall, and recognition occurs at the level of invariant forms. Invariant form refers to the brain's internal representation of an external form. This representation does not change even though the stimuli informing you it's there are in a constant state of flux (Hawkins and Blakeslee 2004).

A 1993 study at the University of Vienna revealed the extent to which different regions of the human brain cooperate when composing music (this also occurred in some listeners). Professor Hellmuth Petsche and his associates determined that brain-wave coherence occurred at many sites throughout the cerebral cortex (Petsche 1993). For some forms of music, the correlation between the left and right frontal lobes increases, that is, brain waves become more similar between the frontal lobes of the two hemispheres (Tatsuya, Mitsuo, and Tadao 1997). For example, in a study involving exposure of four-year-old children to one hour of music per day over a six-month period, brain bioelectric activity data indicated an enhancement of the coherence function (Flohr, Miller, and DeBeus 2000).

In a study of the relationship of coherence and degree of musical training, subjects with music training exhibited significantly more EEG coherence within and between hemispheres than those without such training in a control group (Johnson et al. 1996).[2] In other words, it appeared musical training increased the number of functional interconnections in the brain. Specifically, the researchers suggested that greater coherence in musicians "may reflect a specialized organization of brain activity in subjects with music training for enabling the experiences of ordered acoustic patterns" (Johnson et al. 1996, 582).

Further, in a study of thirty professional classical musicians and thirty non-musician controls matched for age, sex, and handedness, MRI scans revealed that there was a positive relationship between corpus callosum size and the number of fibers crossing through it, indicating a difference in interhemispheric communication between musicians and controls (Schlaug et al. 1995; Springer and Deutsch 1997). In other words, the two hemispheres of the brains of the musicians had a larger number of connections than those of the control group. Thus, as Jensen confirms, "Music ... may be a valuable tool for the integration of thinking across both brain hemispheres" (Jensen 2000b, 246). And as summed up by Thompson, brain function is enhanced through increased cross-callosal communication between the two hemispheres of the brain (Thompson 2007).

Musicians have structural changes that are "profound and seemingly permanent" (Sousa 2006, 224). As Sousa describes, "the auditory cortex, the motor cortex, the cerebellum, and the corpus callosum are larger in musicians than in non-musicians" (2006, 224). This, of course, moves beyond being able to discern different tonal and visual patterns to acquiring new motor skills. Since the brains of musicians and non-musicians are structurally different—yet studies of five- to seven-year-olds beginning music lessons show no pre-existing differences (Restak 2003; Sousa 2006; Norton et al. 2005)—it appears that most musicians are made, not born. An example is perfect pitch, the ability to name individual tones. Perfect pitch is not an inherited phenomenon. Restak (2003) discovered that perfect pitch can be acquired by average children between three and five years of age when given appropriate training. Structural brain changes occur along with the development of perfect pitch and continue as musical talent matures (Restak 2003).

We have now answered two of our introductory questions: listening to music regularly (along with replaying tunes in our brains) helps keep our neurons and synapses active and alive; listening to the right music does appear to facilitate learning; further, participating more fully in music making appears to provide additional cerebral advantages. But, as we will discover, some music offers an even greater opportunity to heighten our conscious awareness in terms of sensory inputs, expand our awareness of, and access to, that which we have gathered and stored in our unconscious, and grow and expand our mental capacity and capabilities.

Since music has its own frequencies, it can either resonate or be in conflict with the body's rhythms. The pulse (heartbeat) of the listener tends to synchronize with the beat of the music being heard (the faster the music, the faster the heartbeat). When this resonance occurs, the individual learns better. As Jensen confirms, "When both are resonating on the same frequency, we fall 'in sync,' we learn better, and we're more aware and alert" (Jensen 2000b). This is a starting point for further exploring brain coherence.

Hemispheric Synchronization

Hemispheric synchronization is the use of sound coupled with a binaural beat to bring both hemispheres of the brain into unison (Bennet and Bennet 2007). Binaural beats were identified in 1839 by H. W. Dove, a German experimenter. In the human mind, binaural beats are detected with carrier tones (audio tones of slightly different frequencies, one to each ear) below approximately 1500 Hz (Oster 1973). The mind perceives the frequency differences of the sound coming into each ear, mixing the two sounds to produce a fluctuating rhythm and thereby creating a beat or difference frequency. Because each side of the body sends signals to the opposite hemisphere of the brain, both hemispheres must work together to "hear" the difference frequency.

This perceived rhythm originates in the brain stem (Oster 1973) and is neurologically routed to the reticular formation (Swann et al. 1982), then moves to the cortex where it can be measured as a frequency-following response (Hink et al. 1980; Marsh, Brown, and Smith 1975; Smith et al. 1978). This interhemispheric communication is the setting for brain-wave coherence, which facilitates whole-brain cognition (Ritchey 2003), that is, an integration of left- and right-brain functioning (Carroll 1986).

What can occur during hemispheric synchronization is a physiologically reduced state of arousal while maintaining conscious awareness (Atwater 2004; Fischer 1971; Delmonte 1984; Goleman 1988; Jevning, Wallace, and Beidenbach 1992; Mavromatis 1991; West 1980) and the capacity to reach the unconscious creative state described above through the window of consciousness. In an exploration of tacit knowledge published in VINE at the beginning of 2008, the authors introduced the use of sound as an approach to accessing tacit knowledge. For example, listening to a special song in your life can draw out deep feelings and memories buried in your unconscious. Further, interhemispheric communication was introduced as a setting for achieving brain-wave coherence (a doorway into the unconscious), providing greater access to knowledge (informing) and knowledge (proceeding), thereby facilitating learning (Bennet and Bennet 2008). By reference the ideas forwarded in that work are included here.

In 1971 Robert Monroe—an engineer, founder of The Monroe Institute® and arguably the leading pioneer of achieving learning through expanded forms of consciousness—developed audiotapes with specific beat frequencies that support synchronized, rhythmic patterns of consciousness called Hemi-Sync®. Repeated experiments occurred with individual brain activity observed. The following correlations between brain waves and consciousness were used: beta waves (approximately 13–26 Hz) and focused alertness and increased analytical capabilities; alpha waves (approximately 8–13 Hz) and unfocused alertness; theta waves (approximately 4–8 Hz) and a deep relaxation; and delta waves (approximately 0.5–4 Hz) and deep sleep. While it was discovered that theta waves provided the best learning state and beta waves the best problem-solving state, this posed a problem. Theta is the state of short duration right before and right after sleep (Monroe Institute 1985). This problem was solved by superimposing a beta signal on the theta, which produced a relaxed alertness (Bullard 2003).

This is consistent with the findings from neurobiological research that efficient learning is related to a decrease in brain activation often accompanied by a shift of activation from the prefrontal regions to those regions relevant to the processing of particular tasks (the phenomenon known as the anterior-posterior shift).

The first Metamusic® to combine theta and beta waves (*Remembrance* by J. S. Epperson) was released in 1994 (Bullard 2003). A second Metamusic® piece combining theta and beta waves, released that same year (*Einstein's Dream*, also by Epperson), was based on a modification of Mozart's Sonata for Two Pianos in D Major, the same piece used in the initial study which produced the controversial Mozart effect. This version, however, had embedded combinations of sounds to encourage whole-brain coherence.

Thus, Robert Monroe was developing and releasing audiotapes (and then CDs) specifically designed to help the left and right hemispheres of the brain work together, resulting in increased concentration, learning, and memory (Jensen 2000b). While the range and number of similar music products has expanded over the past years, the many years of both scientific and anecdotal evidence available about the use of Hemi-Sync® provides a plethora of material from which to explore the benefits of brain coherence as it relates to learning. Thus we will briefly explore the context around this technology.

The Hemi-Sync® Experience

There are dozens of recorded studies dated during the 1980s that looked at the relationship of Hemi-Sync® and learning, some specifically focused on educational applications. In 1982, for example, students in the basic broadcasters' course (BBC) of the Defense Information School (DINFOS) at Fort Benjamin Harrison, Indiana, "displayed a number of positive differences in stress reactions and performance responses" over the control groups (Waldkoetter 1991). In a general psychology class, Edrington (1983) discovered that students who listened to verbal information (definitions and terms peculiar to the field of psychology) with a Hemi-Sync® background signal ($4 \pm .2$ Hz) scored significantly higher than the control group on five of six tests.

In 1986, Dr. Gregory Carroll presented the results of a study on the effectiveness of hemispheric synchronization of the brain as a learning tool in the identification of musical intervals. While the results of the experimental group were 5.54 percent higher than the control group, this was not considered significant. A surprise finding, however, was that individuals in the experimental group had a tendency to achieve higher scores on their posttests than on their pretests. The effect was in both the number of individuals and the amount of individual change. Only 28 percent of the individual responses in the control group posttests were higher than their pretests, while 54 percent of the experimental group did much better (Carroll, 1986). This suggests that Hemi-Sync® signals sustained their levels of concentration during the course of the forty-minute tape sessions considerably longer than what occurred (when it occurred) in the Mozart effect studies.

Hemi-Sync® has consistently proven effective in improving enriched learning environments through sensory integration (Morris 1990), enhanced memory (Kennerly 1996), and improved creativity (Hiew 1995) as well as increasing concentration and focus (Atwater 2004; Bullard 2003). There is also a large body of observational research. For example, after fourteen years of using music as part of his practice, medical doctor Brian Dailey found that the use of sound (specifically, Hemi-Sync®) not only had a therapeutic effect for his patients with a variety of illnesses, but could be extremely effective in assisting healthy individuals with concentration, insight, intuition, creativity, and meditation (Mason 2004). This short review has not included the many studies specifically addressing the impact of music, and in particular Hemi-Sync®, on patients with brain damage or learning disorders, which is outside the focus of this paper.

In a recent study on the benefits of long-term participation in The Monroe Institute programs[4] involving more than seven hundred self-selected participants,[5] it was shown that greater experience with Hemi-Sync® increased self-efficacy and life satisfaction (Danielson 2008) at a state of development similar to that of self-transforming (Kegan 1982). As described in the research results,

Individuals at this stage of development recognize the limitations in any perspective and more willingly engage others for the challenge it poses to their worldview as the means for growing more expansive in their experiences—to consciously grow beyond where they are rather than merely having it happen to them as a function of circumstances (Danielson 2008, 25).

The seven hundred study participants (all adults) were evenly divided between single-program participation (SPP) and multiple-program participation (MPP) (indicating increased usage over a longer period of time). SPP means one week of continuous emersion using Hemi-Sync® technology; MPP means multiple weeks of continuous emersion, separated by time periods ranging from weeks to years. Following their Hemi-Sync® experiences, participants reported remarkable results. For example, the following percentages of participants strongly agreed (on a five-point Likert scale) to the following statements:

"I have a more expansive vision of how the parts of my life relate to a whole" (25.29% SPP, 61.3% MPP)

"I am actively involved in my own personal development" (30.65% SPP, 62.45% MPP)

"I take actions that are more true to my sense of self" (18.77% SPP, 45.21% MPP)

"I have been able to resolve an important issue or challenge in my life" (11.88% SPP, 32.57% MPP)

"I am more productive at work" (4.6% SPP, 14.18% MPP)

"I have a clear sense of further development I need to accomplish" (29.5% SPP, 40.23% MPP)

"I am more successful in my career" (6.56% SPP, 17.97% MPP)

Clearly, Hemi-Sync® supports a long-term development program for "those interested in playing on the boundaries of human growth and development ... who want to see positive change in their lives" (Danielson 2008, 25).

Final Thoughts

At a dozen places on the Internet, neurologist Jerre Levy of the University of Chicago[6] is credited with saying (paraphrased) that great men and women of history do not merely have superior intellectual capacities within each hemisphere of the brain. They also have phenomenal levels of emotional commitment, motivation, and attentional capacity, all of which reflect the highly integrated brain in action.

As we have seen, for the past thirty years, and perhaps longer, there have been studies in the mainstream touting the connections between music and mind/brain activity (from the viewpoints of psychology, music, education, etc.), and another expanding set of studies not as mainstream (from the viewpoint of consciousness). As our thought and understanding as a species is expanding, these areas of focus are openly acknowledging each other and learning together. It is no longer necessary or desirable to limit our thoughts to one frame of reference, nor to place boundaries on our mental capacity and ability to expand or contract that capacity.

We have seen evidence that changes in brain organization and function occur with the acquisition of musical skills. From the external viewpoint, whether as a listener or participant, music clearly offers the potential to strengthen and increase the interconnections across the hemispheres of the brain. As an example, the sound technology of Hemi-Sync® offers the potential to achieve brain coherence, thus facilitating whole-brain cognition.

This is not to say that sound—music, Mozart, or Hemi-Sync®—offers a panacea for learning. Let's not produce the disappointment of creating a meme without context. When asked what to expect from the Hemi-Sync® experience, engineer and developer Robert Monroe responded,

As much or as little as you put into it. Some discover themselves and thus live more completely, more constructively. Others reach levels of awareness so profound that one such experience is enough for a lifetime. Still others become seekers-after-truth and add an on-going adventure to their daily activity (Monroe 2007).

We've come full circle. Learning is occurring in the mind/brain as long as there is life; this is part of the inheritance of Darwinian survival of the fittest. But the amount, quality, and direction of that learning, and the environments in which we live, are choices. Yes, Charles Darwin, regularly listening to music—and, even better, participating in music making—would have undoubtedly kept more neurons alive and active, and synapses intact.

Now our opportunity is to fully exploit this understanding in our organizations, in our communities, and in our everyday lives.

Appendix B End Notes

[1] The terms coherence and entrainment are often interchanged. Entrainment, however, is used to describe a form of coherence achieved when two or more body systems are synchronous and operating at the same frequency. For example, at HeartMath® the term entrainment is used to describe this relationship between the respiration and heart-rhythm patterns.

[2] It was also found that females had higher coherence than males, which is in accord with anatomical studies showing that females have a larger number of interhemispheric connections than males.

[3] While used as a short term for hemispheric synchronization, Hemi-Sync® is also the term patented by Robert Monroe to describe the Hemi-Sync® auditory-guidance system, a binaural-beat sound technology that demonstrated changes in focused states of consciousness in over thirty years of study.

[4] "The Benefits of long-term participation in the Monroe Institute programs" was released in early 2008 by The Monroe Institute.

[5] More than twenty thousand people worldwide have participated in formal Hemi-Sync® programs at the Institute. An equivalent number of people have participated in OUTREACH programs, which are conducted in English, Spanish, French, German, and Japanese.

[6] Levy is a strong debunker of the left brain/right brain myth (Levy 1985).

Appendix B References

Abeles, H. F., and E. M. Sanders. 2005. Final assessment report: New Jersey Symphony Orchestra's Early Strings Program. New York: Center for Arts Education Research, Columbia University.

Amen, D. G. 2005. *Making a good brain great*. New York: Harmony Books.

Atwater, F. H. 2004. *The Hemi-Sync process*. Faber, VA: The Monroe Institute.

Begley, S. 2007. *Train your mind, change your brain*. New York: Ballantine Books.

Bennet, A., and D. Bennet. 2000. *Knowledge mobilization in the social sciences and humanities: Moving from research to action*. Frost, WV: MQI Press.

Bennet, D., and A. Bennet. 2008. *Engaging tacit knowledge in support of organizational learning*. VINE 38 (1): 72–94.

Bullard, B. 2003. *METAMUSIC: Music for inner space*, Hemi-Sync Journal 21 (3–4): 1–5.

Campbell, D. 2000. *Heal yourself with sound and music*. Boulder, CO: Sounds True.

Carroll, G. D. 1986. Brain hemisphere synchronization and musical learning. Unpublished paper. University of North Carolina at Greensboro.

Catterall, J., R. Chapleau, and J. Iwanga. 1999. Involvement in the arts and human development: Extending an analysis of general associations and introducing the special cases of intense involvement in music and in theater arts. Monograph Series No. 11. Washington, DC: Americans for the Arts.

Chabris, C. 1999. A quantitative meta-analysis of Mozart studies. Nature 400:826–27.

Chugani, H. T. 1998. Biological basis of emotion: Brain systems and brain development. Pediatrics 102 (5): 1225–29.

Clynes, M., ed. 1982. *Music, mind, and brain*. New York: Plenum Press.

Coch, D., K. W. Fischer, and G. Dawson, eds. 2007. *Human behavior, learning, and the developing brain: Typical development*. New York: The Guilford Press.

Cohen, D., R. Granot, H. Pratt, and A. Barneah. 1993. Cognitive meanings of musical elements as disclosed by event-related potential (ERP) and verbal experiments. Music Perception 5 (11): 153–84.

Danielson, C. 2008. Final report: The benefits of long-term participation in The Monroe Institute programs. Faber, VA: The Monroe Institute. See www.monroeinstitute.org/journal/the-benefits-of-long-term-participation-in-tmi-programs

Delmonte, M. M. 1984. Electrocortical activity and related phenomena associated with meditation practice: A literature review. International Journal of Neuroscience 24:217–31.

Dobbs, D. 2007. Turning off depression. In *Best of the brain from Scientific American: Mind, matter, and tomorrow's brain*, ed. F. E. Bloom. New York: Dana Press.

Edelman, G. 1992. *Bright air, brilliant fire*. New York: Basic Books.

Edrington, D. 1983. Hypermnesia experiment. Breakthrough, September. Faber, VA: The Monroe Institute of Applied Sciences.

Fagan, J., J. Prigot, M. Carroll, L. Pioli, A. Stein, and A. Franco. 1997. Auditory context and memory retrieval in young infants. Child Development 68:1057–66.

Felix, U. 1993. The contribution of background music to the enhancement of learning in Suggestopedia: A critical review of the literature. Journal of the Society for Accelerative Learning and Teaching 18 (3–4): 277–303.

Fischer, R. 1971. A cartography of ecstatic and meditative states. Science 174 (4012): 897–904.

Flohr, J., D. Miller, and R. DeBeus. 2000. EEG studies with young children. Music Educators Journal 87 (2): 28–32.

Godden, D. R., and A. D. Baddeley. 1975. Context-dependent memory in two natural environments: On land and underwater. British Journal of Psychology 66:325–31.

Goleman, G. M. 1988. *The meditative mind: The varieties of meditative experience*. New York: G. P. Putnam.

Graziano, A. B., M. Peterson, and G. L. Shaw. 1999. Enhanced learning of proportional math through music training and spatial-temporal training. Neurological Research 21:139–52.

Hallom, S. 2002. The effects of background music on studying. Pp. 74-75 in Critical links: Learning in the arts and student academic and social development, ed. R. J. Deasy. Washington, DC: Arts Education Partnership.

Hannon, E. E., and S. P. Johnson. 2005. Infants use meter to categorize rhythms and melodies: Implications for musical structure learning. Cognitive Psychology 50:354–77.

Hawkins, J., with S. Blakeslee. 2004. On intelligence: How a new understanding of the brain will lead to the creation of truly intelligent machines. New York: Times Books.

Hetland, L. 2000. Listening to music enhances spatial-temporal reasoning: Evidence for the "Mozart Effect." Journal of Aesthetic Education 34:105–48.

Hiew, C. C. 1995. Hemi-Sync into creativity. Hemi-Sync Journal 13 (1): 3–5.

Hink, R. F., K. Kodera, O. Yamada, K. Kaga, and J. Suzuki. 1980. Binaural interaction of a beating frequency- following response. Audiology 19 (1): 36–43.

Ho, Y.-C., M-C. Cheung, and A. S. Chan. 2003. Music training improves verbal but not visual memory: Cross sectional and longitudinal explorations in children. Neuropsychology 17:439–50.

Hodges, D. 2000. Implications of music and brain research. Music Educators Journal 87 (2): 17–22.

Hughes, J. R., J. J. Fino, and M. A. Melyn. 1999. Is there a chronic change of the "Mozart effect" on epileptiform activity? A case study. Clinical Electroencephalography 30:44–45.

Jensen, E. 2000b. Brain-based learning: The new science of teaching and training. San Diego, CA: The Brain Store.

Jensen, E. 2002. Environments for learning. Thousand Oaks, CA: Corwin Press.

Jevning, R., R. K. Wallace, and M. Beidenbach. 1992. The physiology of meditation: A review. Neuroscience and Behavioral Reviews 16:415–24.

Johnson, J. D., C. W. Cotman, C. S. Tasaki, and G. L. Shaw. 1998. Enhancement of spatial-temporal reasoning after a Mozart listening condition in Alzheimer's disease: A case study. Neurology Research 20:666–72.

Johnson, J. K., H. Petsche, P. Richter, A. Von Stein, and O. Filz. 1996. The dependence of coherence estimates of spontaneous EEG on gender and music training. Music Perception 13:563–82.

Kay, A. 2000. Effective music education. Teaching Music 7 (8): 51–53.

Kegan, R. 1982. The evolving self. Boston: Harvard University Press.

Kennerly, R. C. 1996. An empirical investigation into the effect of beta frequency binaural beat audio signals on four measures of human memory. Hemi-Sync Journal 14 (3): 1–4. http://www.monroeinstitute.org/wiki/index.php/An_Empirical_Investigation_Into_the_Effect_of_Beta_Frequency_Binaural_Beat_Audio_Signals_on_Four_Measures_of_Human_Memory (accessed June 20, 2008).

King, J. 1991. Comparing alpha induction differences between two music samples. Abstract from the Center for Research on Learning and Cognition, University of North Texas.

Levy, J. 1985. Right brain, left brain: Fact and fiction. Psychology Today, May, 43.

Lozanov, G. 1991. On some problems of the anatomy, physiology, and biochemistry of cerebral activities in the global-artistic approach in modern Suggestopedagogic training. Journal of the Society for Accelerative Learning and Teaching 16 (2): 101–16.

Marsh, J. T., W. S. Brown, and J. C. Smith. 1975. Far-field recorded frequency-following responses: Correlates of low pitch auditory perception in humans. Electroencephalography and Clinical Neurophysiology 38:113–19.

Mason, R. 2004. The sound medicine of Brian Dailey, M.D., F.A.C.E.P. Alternative and Complementary Therapies 10 (3): 156–60.

Mavromatis, A. 1991. Hypnagogia. New York: Routledge.

Monroe, R. 2007. Quote in The Hemi-Sync® catalog. Faber, VA: Monroe Products.

Monroe Institute. 1985. Achieving optimal learning states. Breakthrough, March. Faber, VA: The Monroe Institute.

Morris, S. E. 1990. Hemi-Sync and the facilitation of sensory integration. Hemi-Sync Journal 8 (4): 5–6.

Muftuler, L. T., M. Bodner, G. L. Shaw, and O. Nalcioglu. 1999. fMRI of Mozart effect using auditory stimuli. Abstract presented at the 87th meeting of the International Society for Magnetic Resonance in Medicine, Philadelphia.

Nakamura, S., N. Sadato, T. Oohashi, E. Nishina, Y. Fuwamoto, and Y. Yonekura. 1999. Analysis of music-brain interaction with simultaneous measurement of regional cerebral blood flow and electroencephalogram beta rhythm in human subjects. Neuroscience Letters 275 (3): 222–26.

Norton, A., E. Winner, K. Cronin, K. Overy, D. J. Lee, and G. Schlaug. 2005. Are there pre-existing neural, cognitive, or motoric markers for musical ability? Brain and Cognition 59:124–34.

Oster, G. 1973. Auditory beats in the brain. Scientific American 229:94–102.

Petsche, H. 1993. Brainwave coherence. Music Perception 11:117–51.

Rauscher, F. H., G. L. Shaw, and K. N. Ky. 1993. Music and spatial task performance. Nature 365:611.

Rauscher, F. H., G. L. Shaw, and K. N. Ky. 1995. Listening to Mozart enhances spatial-temporal reasoning: Towards a neurophysiological basis. Neuroscience Letters 185 (1): 44–47.

Rauscher, F. H., G. L. Shaw, L. J. Levine, E. L. Wright, W. R. Dennis, and R. L. Newcomb. 1997. Music training causes long-term enhancement of preschool children's spatial-temporal reasoning. Neurological Research 19:2–8.

Restak, R. M. 2003. The new brain: How the modern age is rewiring your mind. New York: Rodale.

Rideout, B. E., and C. M. Laubach. 1996. EEG correlates of enhanced spatial performance following exposure to music. Perceptual and Motor Skills 82 (2): 427–32.

Rideout, B. E., and J. Taylor. 1997. Enhanced spatial performance following 10 minutes exposure to music: A replication. Perceptual and Motor Skills 85 (1): 112–14.

Rideout, B. E., S. Dougherty, and L. Wernert. 1998. Effect of music on spatial performance: A test of generality. Perceptual and Motor Skills 86 (2): 512–14.

Ritchey, D. 2003. The H.I.S.S. of the A.S.P.: Understanding the anomalously sensitive person. Terra Alta, WV: Headline Books.

Schlaug, G., L. Jancke, Y. Huang, J. Staiger, and H. Steinmetz. 1995. Increased corpus callosum size in musicians. Neuropsychologia 33:1047–55.

Schmithhorst, V. J., and S. K. Holland. 2004. The effect of musical training on the neural correlates of math processing: A functional magnetic resonance imaging study in humans. Neuroscience Letters 354:193–96.

Smith, J. C., J. T. Marsh, S. Greenberg, and W. S. Brown. 1978. Human auditory frequency-following responses to a missing fundamental. Science 201:639–41.

Soundlab. 2005. http://soundlab.cs.princeton.edu/learning/tutorials/SoundVoice/sndvoic2.htm (accessed May 26, 2008).

Sousa, D. A. 2006. How the brain learns. 3rd ed. Thousand Oaks, CA: Corwin Press.

Springer, S. P., and G. Deutsch. 1997. Left brain, right brain: Perspectives from cognitive neuroscience. New York: W. H. Freeman and Co.

Steele, K. M., J. D. Brown, and J. A. Stoecker. 1999. Failure to confirm the Rauscher and Shaw description of recovery of the Mozart effect. Perceptual and Motor Skills 88 (1): 843–49.

Swain, J. 1997. Musical languages. New York: W. W. Norton.

Swann, R., S. Bosanko, R. Cohen, R. Midgley, and K. M. Seed. 1982. The brain: A user's manual. New York: G. P. Putnam and Sons.

Tatsuya, I., H. Mitsuo, and H. Tadao. 1997. Changes in alpha band EEG activity in the frontal area after stimulation with music of different affective content. Perceptual and Motor Skills 84 (2): 515–26.

Thompson, J. D. 2007. Acoustic brainwave entrainment with binaural beats. http://www.neuroacoustic.com/entrainment.html (accessed June 16, 2008).

Tomatis, A. 1983. Brain/mind bulletin collections. New Sense Bulletin 8, no. 4A (Jan. 24).

Vaughn, K. 2000. Music and mathematics: Modest support for the oft-claimed relationships. Journal of Aesthetic Education 34 (3–4): 149–66.

Waldkoetter, R. O. 1991. Hemi-Sync uses in military settings: Education and counseling</a>. Hemi-Sync Journal 9 (4): 11–12.

Webb, D., and T. Webb. 1990. Accelerated learning with music. Norcross, GA: Accelerated Learning Systems.

Weinberger, N. M. 1995. Nonmusical outcomes of music education. MuSICA Research Notes 2 (2): 6.

Weinberger, N. M. 1999. Can music really improve the mind? The question of transfer effects. MuSICA Research Notes 5 (6): 12.

Weinberger, N. M. 2004. Music and the brain. Scientific American 291:89–95.

West, M. A. 1980. Meditation and the EEG. Psychological Medicine 10:369–75.

Wilson, F. 1991. Music and the neurology of time. Music Educators Journal 77 (5): 26–30.

Wilson, T. L., and T. L. Brown. 1997. Reexamination of the effect of Mozart's music on spatial-task performance. Journal of Psychology 131 (4): 365–70.

Zatorre, R. 1997. Hemispheric specialization of human auditory processing: Perception of speech and musical sounds. Advances in Psychology 123:299.

Zull, J. E. 2002. The art of changing the brain: Enriching the practice of teaching by exploring the biology of learning. Sterling, VA: Stylus.

Appendix C

Movement and Sound:

The Orchestrated Dance in the Brain
That Facilitates Whole Brain Learning

Carmen Montoto

[This paper introduces the relationship among Brain Gym® and Hemi-Sync®, discusses research in this area, and provides examples of their combined use in an educational setting.]

You cannot separate sound from movement. In the music of their eternal dance, matter is created and transformed. Nature in its perennial wisdom recreates this in the brain. The human body is a reflection of the Universe and what occurs in the macro occurs in micro.

Entirely embedded in bone is the labyrinth of the inner ear, where sound and movement are processed together, sound in the cochlea and movement in the three canals.

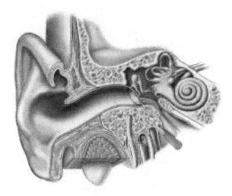

They are part of the Cochlear- Vestibular System, which is considered by Dr. Alfred Tomatis as the dynamo of the brain and the threshold to whole brain learning (Tomatis, 1987). Tomatis proved that auditory stimulation affects the voice, language acquisition, movement coordination, posture, cognition (comprehension and memory) and sensory integration

Fascinatingly, as soon as the heart is created in the human embryo, the ear starts developing to "hear" its beat. The ear is critical to learning.

The Vestibular System:

(1) Serves as the link between the inner and the outer world, allowing for both inner and outer communication.

(2) Helps us to focus and concentrate by cutting off irrelevant stimuli. Helps us sort and organize information into meaningful hierarchies.

(3) Allows us to stand upright, maintain balance and move through space.

(4) Continuously and automatically adjusts heart rate and blood pressure.

(5) Maintains the muscle tone and limb position.

(6) Plays an important role in sensory integration, processing and organizing what we perceive through the senses.

(7) Coordinates information from the vestibular organs in the inner ear, the eyes, muscles and joints, fingertips and palms of the hands, pressure on the soles of the feet, jaw, and gravity receptors on the skin.

Sound affects matter, emotions, cognition, consciousness and health. The work of Dr. Hans Jenny, Cymatics, demonstrates the impact sound has on matter (Jenny, 1967). Dr. Masaru Emoto's pictures on water crystals shows the effect sound; words and music have on water (Emoto, 2001). If we consider the fact that we are 70 percent water, the planet earth is 70 percent water we become aware of the importance of his findings.

Aristotle and Plato realized the effect music has on cognition and emotional states. Their findings have been validated by many studies that attest on how the brain processes information and learns. Music is processed in the limbic system and the frontal cortex, affecting memory and comprehension. As demonstrated by the research done at TMI, sound can synchronize the brain, enhancing its cognitive functions and potential. Sound and music can be used to explore altered states of consciousness and expand our intuition.

In Allopathic medicine ultrasound frequencies are being used to dissolve bladder stones and sonograms for accurate diagnostics. Various instruments and therapies had been created around sound healing in alternative medicine. The use of music in healing included Root Frequency, Sound Healing with the Voice, the Neurophone, Tuning Fork Treatment, Bells, Hydro Acoustic Therapy, Tibetan/Crystal Bowl Massage, and the Hado Scan.

A Sound Journey:

An Introduction to Hemi Sync

In 1999 I used Hemi-Sync® tapes for the first time, specifically, Transcendence, A Mind Food exercise specifically designed to help listeners turn inward in support of a powerful meditative journey. This experience triggered an out of body experience. Surprised by the amazing results, I decided to put attending an in-house session at The Monroe Institute (TMI) in my priority list and give it a try.

The Gateway Program was an extra-ordinary experience. It gave "North" to my life in a moment where I needed a new direction. To expand my understanding of the Hemi-Sync® process and experience, I bought several tapes and met with my friends once a week to do exercises. We all started seeing astounding results. A friend of mine that was going through a depression because of the death of her husband started feeling better, others were expanding their intuition, and I noticed that my thinking seemed to be more integrated and focused If all that we were experiencing could be replicated, then Hemi-Sync® could be an important tool in people's life, and could potentially take learning and education to another level, helping children to learn faster. This was the beginning of a "sound" journey, an experience that continues to enrich my life, and the lives of my family, friends and those whom I meet in Puerto Rico and abroad.

Since 2002 Hemi-Sync® has been used in schools to enhance learning in Puerto Rico. It started in Montessori and continued in private and public schools. That same year I became a member of the Professional Division at TMI and attended my first

Professional Division Meeting. The presentations provided insights on the diversified applications of this wonderful technology, some of which we were experiencing and others that were previously unknown to me. I read all the research that I could lay my hands on about the use of Hemi Sync in learning, and took a course on photo reading to expand the possibilities. The use of the *Concentration* CD with headphones made a positive difference on me and with several students that gave it a try in the photo reading class. *Concentration* is a non-verbal Mind Food offering, that is perfect for any mental task requiring focus and concentration. It can serve as a background piece while performing mental tasks such as studying, reading, or working on a computer.

In those early days, to improve the reading skills of the students in the schools a combination of photo reading techniques and Hemi-Sync® was used. Teachers were presented with copies of some of the research papers from TMI and the principals with the work of D. Edrington. He was an early writer (1983 1984) on the attention, and hypermnesia and the use of Hemi-Sync®. His work is available in the newsletters and journals of TMI.

Visiting schools made me aware of the medications that were being used to treat children with ADD and ADHD, and of the growth of autism in Puerto Rico and around the world. Teachers in the Public Educational System could force parents to have their children evaluated—and then medicated—when a student displayed disruptive conduct in the classroom. In the presentations offered in schools parents and teachers asked if Hemi-Sync® could help these children. I said yes and send copies of the studies performed by TMI Professional Division members such as Robert Sorsons, Barbara Bullard, Jacqueline Mast and Susan Evan Morris. Many chose to try Hemi-Sync®

Early Hemi-Sync® Feedback

Feedback from the parents and teachers using the CDs was very positive. One teacher that did tutoring had two dyslexic students. By the end of the semester their problem was gone, they were writing and reading perfectly. A mother of an autistic child gave Remembrance to a third grade teacher in a Special Education School. At the end of the month the students themselves recognized that they were doing much better, and asked her to put the music on all the time. The teacher described the students as more focused and more relaxed, and they were getting better grades! Parents were having similar results in the home. Children of various ages wanted their parents to "play the music that made them learn easier."

At that time the CDs recommended were *Remembrance, Baroque Garden, Einstein's Dream, Midsummer Night*, and *Masterworks*. For parents using Hemi-Sync® in the home, *Cloudscape* and *Sleeping through the Rain* were added for sleep and relaxation, for memory *Retain-Recall-Release* and *Buy the Numbers* for math. Buy the Numbers proved to be very effective with Middle School and High School students. A High School student come into my office on a Friday, the weekend before his final math exam which would determine if he had to take remedial classes during the summer. He bought a *Pal Student* CD set and *Buy the Numbers*, used them regularly for three days in addition to studying with *Concentration* in the background, and instead of spending his summer in remedial classes he went with his family on vacations. Needless to say we were all elated.

The results on special education students demonstrated the positive effect sound had on cognition and sensory integration.

In many of the materials I read about hemispheric synchronization and the use of sound, the name of Robert Monroe and Hemi-Sync® kept reappearing. This assured me that I was in the right track. The Mega Brain by Hutchinson, The Power of Sound by Joshua Leeds, the work by Jonathan Goldman, and dozens of other articles and publications mentioned Monroe. At this point I was convinced that **sound affects our mind, health and spirit.** Further, I had discovered that these findings were cross-cultural, and have scientific and experiential research to validate them.

In 2003 I became an Outreach Instructor for The Monroe Institute.

Expanding the Use of Hemi-Sync®

Because of the importance of sleep to health and cognition, a sleep CD was added to the learning Hemi-Sync® CDs to reinforce the effects students were experiencing. For example, students studying for final exams and board tests have sleep issues. In addition, many of the children and adults with ADD, ADHD, and Autism go to sleep late and don't relax themselves when sleeping. As a mother of an autistic child said to me, "When my 8-year-old son slept with *Cloudscape* it was the first time he had slept with his arms and legs extended and not curled in a fetal position."

With the addition of a sleep CD, students were more relaxed and the positive effects were occurring faster. Autistic children that had speech problems were able to expand and improve their vocabulary in short periods of time. For example, there was a two-year-old child who could only say single syllables. After sleeping with *Cloudscapes* one night, he greeted his mother and father the following morning saying "mamá" and "papa." Another example is a 10 year old autistic child who could not add 1 plus 1 without an abacus or similar objects. After sleeping one night with *Cloudscapes* and using *Remembrance* with headphones the next day, he started adding, and has not needed to use an abacus since. Searching for an explanation of why these improvements were occurring, I found studies indicating that neural connections can be strengthened during nighttime.

There have been a number of lessons learned along the way. For example, **I do not recommend the use of headphones on autistic children**. Some of them are very sensitive to anything pressing against them, and similar results can occur with or without earphones. **I also noticed that if we changed the pair of CDs (for sleep and concentration) after 3 months it is more effective.** In some children the need for change comes faster, perhaps even once a month, while in other, they might be fine for 5 months, so 3 months is a middle ground. While I am not sure why this occurs, I have several ideas. One, people get tired of hearing the same music. Two, the brain needs new stimulus to grow. Three, changing the music forces you into a new space, and that's what learning is all about. Life is about change and exploring new possibilities.

Brain Gym® and Hemi-Sync®

In 2007 Salvador Tió, Ruth Reyes, and myself organized with Jacqueline Mast from the Mast Clinic the Eight International Special Education Conference in Puerto Rico. The presenters included professors from Harvard as well as doctors, teachers, lawyers, psychologists, TMI Professional Members, nutritionists, chemists and artists from Puerto Rico and different parts of the world. The parents and teachers that attended obtained tools and new insights to understand and help children and adults with ADD, ADHD, autism, dyslexia and other learning disabilities.

One of the presenters, a teacher, spoke on how Brain Gym® was helping kids in the classroom read and write better. In my head I immediately connected the significance of linking movement and sound. Many of the articles I had read by Sorson, Morrison, and Tomatis reiterated the importance of the vestibular system, specifically, its direct connection with the auditory system, the role it played in sensory integration, and the profound effect this had on whole brain learning. Further, combining movement and sound in an inclusive classroom could help students with learning disabilities as well as regular students. We all need stress reduction and integrating thinking in the world we live in. I went onto the Internet and ended up in Canada taking Brain Gym® 101 with Paul Dennison.

Brain Gym® is educational Kinesiology. It consists of 26 exercises and activities committed to the principle that moving with intention leads to optimal learning. Some of the exercises recall the movements naturally done during the first years of life when learning to coordinate the eyes, ears, hands, and whole body. They were developed by educator and reading specialist Paul E. Dennison, PhD., and his wife and colleague, Gail E. Dennison. Teachers and students have been reporting for over 20 years on the effectiveness of these simple activities. They often bring about dramatic improvements in areas such as reading, writing, math, test taking, physical coordination, concentration, focus, memory relationships, and self-responsibility, attitude and organization skills. The Triune brain model of Paul Mclean is used to explain the three dimensions in which the exercises are categorized: Focus (reptilian brain), Organization (mammalian brain) and Laterality (Neo Cortex). Brain Gym® is a way to relax, make students laugh and expand their potentials.

Returning from Canada, I was eager to test the combination of Brain Gym® and Hemi-Sync®, convinced that the synergies of this combination would take my work to another level. My first experience began the validation of this assumption. A 10 year old child named Javier came to my office. Attempting to use several Brain Gym exercises (Cross Crawls, Brain Buttons, And Lazy Eights), it was evident Javier could not perform these by himself. People with learning disabilities have difficulty coordinating movement and tend to perform the Brain Gym exercises unilaterally, not crossing the mid section of the body. This 10 year old boy had serious academic problems. He was a battered child, and his learning problems were rooted in this situation. When he came to me he had been removed from his parent's home and was under custody of his grandparents. Javier had also been diagnosed as having ADHD and dyslexia. In order to improve his writing skills I did "Lazy Eights" and "Alphabet Eights" with him. These two Brain Gym® exercises have proven to be an effective means to facilitate eye-hand coordination. The "Lazy Eights "is a number eight figure (see Figures A-D) drawn horizontally, the infinity sign. The exercise consists of having the subject draw the sideways eight figure first with his dominant hand, then with the non dominant hand, and thereafter with both hands. At least four times with his eyes open and four times with his eyes closed.

Javier would either get stuck on one side of the Eight or go around the perimeters without crossing the midline as can be seen in Figure A. At this point he was told to write his name. As can be seen in Figure B, he wrote his name with the letters upside down and in the opposite direction. Javier was then asked to use headphones and listen to the Hemi-Sync® *Concentration* CD while the I guided his hand. We then did the "Lazy Eight" and the "Alphabet Eight" exercises up to the letter G together. **The results were remarkable**. Ten minutes later (as can be seen in Figure C) his name was properly written and he was crossing the midline. Further, drawing over the circle is very neat compared to Figure A. The letters inside the circle are there because he misunderstood the instruction of the exercise.

Figure A

Figure B

Figure C

To improve Javier's reading a combination of speed-reading techniques, the *Concentration* CD, and some Brain Gym exercises (the "Elephant" and "PACE") were used. There was a significant improvement in his reading speed and comprehension. As an added benefit, his sister, who also had reading difficulties, practiced the reading exercises with Javier. She was so ecstatic about her own improvement that she gave me a big kiss and a hug when she left. Reading had turned into an easier task for her.

PACE consists of four Brain Gym® movements: *Sipping Water* to energize, improve concentration and hydrate the body; *Brain Buttons* to relax and coordinate eye movement; *Cross Crawls*, a large motor movement that activates both hemispheres and prepares the body for fine motor skills like reading and writing; and *Hook Ups* to center establish equilibrium and bring your presence to the classroom.

Sipping Water   Brain Buttons   Cross Crawls   Hook Ups

In the visits and presentations to the schools PACE was taught along with another Brain Gym exercise that would address the needs of the students. Brain Gym® started spreading into the school system of Puerto Rico.

Research Projects Undertaken

In September 2007 nine Masters Degree students of the Ponce Catholic University in Puerto Rico conducted a study for their master's educational thesis. Under the direction of Professor Ruth Reyes, PhD in Education, these students used Hemi-Sync® to explore how sound enhances learning. On a personal level Professor Reyes had experienced the effect of Hemi-Sync® on her grandchild, and had previously used it in her work. The nine elementary schools participating in the project were public and private catholic school in the southern part of the island located in Adjuntas, Peñuelas, Coamo, Santa Isabel and Ponce. See Figure D.

Figure D

Teachers and faculty members in those nine schools were given a presentation on the effect sound in the brain and how it enhances learning. The specific CDs used in the study were *Angel Paradise, Baroque Garden, Concentration, Einstein's Dream, Illumination, Indigo, Masterworks, Midsummer Night* and *Remembrance*.

The results of this research proved very rewarding. Students improved in reading, writing, math, and conduct! In the school Colegio Nuestra Señora Valvarena in Coamo, the worst behaving first-grade classroom became the best after a month of using Hemi-Sync®.

Realizing the importance **positive affirmations** had on the students coming to my office; in 2008 they were added to the work we were performing. Many of the students I worked with were labelled as having learning problems, ADD, ADHD, Autism, etc. with low self-esteem. These students thought that they were not intelligent. As the positive affirmations were added a routine was created which could be performed by the student before going to school or by the students and teachers in the classroom. In the classroom the teacher would (1) put on the Hemi-Sync® CD; (2) say six or eight affirmations with the students like "I am intelligent", "I am Genius" "I am Healthy", "I am Happy", "I learn easily and understand everything the teacher explains", "I am Peaceful", "I am ......"; and (3) do a PACE with another Brain Gym exercise related to the class that was starting.

A few words about affirmations. Feedback regarding the use of affirmations has been very encouraging. The specific affirmations used are based on the age group. When creating them, it is good for the students to play an active role. Once created, some teachers hang them on strings from the ceiling or simply put them on the walls. In elementary schools they can be made into songs, or for older student they can become part of a rap. In some classrooms, teachers have reported that if they forget to start the day with the affirmations, the students began saying them.

The whole affirmation routine takes around 3 to 5 minutes to do and can dissipate the stress of early rising and morning rush traffic, and create a sense of "I am present to start learning." With the affirmations you reinforce self-esteem; everybody in a given day needs reassurance even those that possess a high self-esteem. Through the use of Hemi-Sync® frequencies, the brain synchronicity occurs and brainwave patterns are created that can support focused attention and learning. By combining PACE as part of the process the body is prepared for whole brain learning, reducing stress and creating a sense of awareness in a fun way.

In 2009 Marilyn Felix, a Doctoral Degree student, from the Metropolitan University of Cupey (UMET), under the supervision of professor Sonia Dávila, PhD, decided to test the results we were getting as part of the investigation she would use for her thesis paper. She was part of a research program called LUVE (La Universidad Va a la Escuela[1]). Felix wanted to prove how sound and movement effects based on neuroscience concepts of how the brain learns could be verified and duplicated.

Felix is the principal of the school Luis Muñoz Rivera in Las Piedras, Puerto Rico. I had visited her school and taught the children and the teachers several Brain Gym® exercises, which got her research project started. As part of this project, Felix supervised the teachers, collected the data, analyzed it, and then published her results. For the study she used a second-grade classroom consisting of sixteen students who had reading problems. At the beginning of the school years these students had taken a standardized oral test that showed their reading skills as below average. After eight weeks of practicing the affirmations, using the Hemi-Sync® music of *Remembrance*, *Masterworks* and *Concentration* in the background, and doing PACE plus other Brain Gym® exercises for reading and writing, the standard test was repeated with an improvement of 52 percent in their oral reading.

At the end of the school year in 2010, the day they gave the standardized test (called La Prueba Puertorriqueña), the whole school practiced several Brain Gym® exercises in the courtyard and Hemi-Sync® was played while the students took the test. The overall student results from this test determine the level the school is placed in the educational system. The 2010 results reflected a 10 percent improvement over the previous year performance.

One second grade teacher bought the *Concentration* CD and played it during the final exam day to her lowest performing group of students. They did better than the best performing group who took the exams without the benefit of Hemi-Sync®. These results replicated the results attained in many other schools in Puerto Rico. It

---

[1] The initials stand for the University that goes to the schools.

was clear that there was a direct link between exam performance and the use of Hemi-Sync®.

Figure E

Figure F

In Figure E students at Luis Muñoz Rivera are practicing speed reading with Hemi-Sync®. In Figure F students at the same school are performing the Brain Gym® exercise called Arm Activation to improve writing.

In the center we created a class called Alambraje® or Wiring where arts (painting and theater) and exercises (Yoga, Tai Chi, and Martial Arts) are added to the Brain Gym® exercises, Hemi-Sync® and positive affirmations. Students come once a week. They take one hour of exercise and then—accompanied by their parents—participate in a half hour class where they learn different Brain Gym® exercises specifically designed to improve their reading, writing and art work. Earlier I introduced the importance of movement and how improvement in gross motor skills has an impact on fine motor skills such as painting, writing and reading.

Getting the parents involved and providing the opportunity for them to try these things out for themselves was very important. Some parents used these tools to improve their reading and writing skills, and some of the parents reported that the Hemi-Sync® CDs enriched and improved other areas of their life. Not only is the experiential approach fun for parents, but also when they discover the process works for them, they are generally more consistent in applying the process with their kids.

Figure G

Figure H

Figure I

Figure J

In Figure G students are doing aerobics as part of the Alambraje® training. In figure H students are in the art class with their parents practicing alphabet eights and double doodles. Figure I is a drawing with the positive affirmations done by a student in the class. Figure J is Performing Night on the play called "The Alambraje Circus".

Continuing Outreach

The combination of Hemi-Sync® with Brain Gym® has attracted the attention of therapist and speech pathologists, opening the door to **Special Education Centers** throughout the island. The results of using Hemi-Sync® and Brain Gym® in these centers have been encouraging. For example, the ESPIVI center in Mayagüez reported excellent results with autistic children. Specifically, the children are more relaxed, alert and focused attributes that are improving their learning capacities and their interpersonal relationships. The current director wants all the therapist and teachers in the center to become versed in the use of Hemi-Sync® and to eventually become Brain Gym® practitioners.

During the period between 2005 and 2010, I continued presenting in many Puerto Rico Universities as well as in Institutions abroad how affirmations, sound and movement enhance the learning process. Several interesting projects are developing thanks to the interest of several university professors who have experienced the results personally or been present to see the results obtained in classrooms throughout the island. In collaboration with the Division of Continuing Education and Professional Studies of the University of Puerto Rico, we are currently designing a course called "Innovative Tools for Learning in the 21st Century" which will include the use of sound, movement, nutrition and NLP on learning. The last module will involve applying these tools with special education students.

In the Central University of Bayamón, under the guidance of Pura Echandi, PhD, head of the educational department, we are creating an experimental course for the university students who are studying to become teachers. These students will use positive affirmations and the Brain Gym® exercises in combination with Hemi-Sync® in the schools where they do their practice. As part of the course, they will collect and analyze resulting data. In the University of PR in Humacao similar research is going to be done on pre-school children.

Further, we are in the process of obtaining education contact hours (CE Contact Hours) and continuing education units (CEUs) for a number of courses involving Brain Gym® and a course I created with the guidance of Carol Sabick, PhD, Director of the trainers program at The Monroe Institute called "The Effect of sound on Cognition."

In 2010 Monroe Products prepared the LEK or *Learning Enhancement Kit.* This Package is the result of the work I had been doing that corroborated the findings of Bullard, Edrington, Sorson, Morris and many other members of the Professional Division at TMI. The LEK can facilitate the learning process of students whether working in a classroom or studying at home. The CDs included in this collection were specifically chosen to create whole brain learning, focused attention, relaxation and the perfect sleep, all important elements to enhance cognitive functions. Designed to promote success and assist all involved in the learning process (teachers, parents, and students of all ages); they are perfect for accelerated learning as well as students with special needs and their parents.

Meeting the Challenge

There is so much to be learned about learning. Emotions, nutrition, relaxation, sleep, visualizations, sound, movement and genetics all affect our capacity to concentrate, memorize, process and understand information. Brain research is changing the paradigm of how neurons work and how we process what is perceived through the senses in different areas of the brain. The discovery of multisensory neurons is shedding a new light on sensory integration and the importance of brain synchronization.

The children of the 21st century are growing up in a technological world that changes very fast. The skills we learn today might be obsolete tomorrow as technology changes and new theories emerge. Rich in opportunities, the challenges demand that we acquire tools and approaches that can help us relax, sleep and learn faster. We must also figure out ways to support the learning needs of a growing population of ADD, ADHD and autistic children, who are rapidly growing into adults. The use of Hemi-Sync® and Brain Gym® seems an excellent combination to further explore.

Appendix C Bibliography

Ayres, A. Jean. *Sensory Integration and Learning Disorders*. Western Psychological Services, Los Angeles, Calif., 1972.

Campbell, Don. *The Mozart Effect*. Avon Books, New York, N.Y., 1997.

Dennison, Paul & Gail. *Brain Gym Teachers Edition*. Edu-Kinesthetics, Inc., Glendale, Calif, 1989 Dennison, Paul. *Brain Gym® and Me Reclaiming the Pleasure of Learning*. Edu-Kinesthetics, Inc., Ventura, Calif., 2006.

Dennison, Paul E. and Gail E Dennison. *Brain Gym:® Simple Activities for Whole Brain Learning*. Edu-Kinesthetics, Ventura, Calif., 1998.

Emoto, Masaru. *The Hidden Messages of Water*. Beyond Words Publishing, Hillsboro, Oregon, 2004. Hannaford, Carla, 1985. *Smart Moves; Why Learning is Not All in Your Head*, (Revised Edition) Great River Books, 2005.

Hannaford, Carla. *The Dominance Factor*. Great River Books, 1997.

Leeds, Joshua. *The Power of Sound* Healing Arts Press Rochester, Vermont, 2001.

Lozanov,George. *Suggestology and Outlines of Suggestopedy* NY, NY. Gordon and Breach Science Publishers 1978 .

Jenny, Hans. *Cymatics, A Study of Wave Phenomena*, (Revised Edition) Newmarket, New Hampshire, 2001.

MacLean, Paul. *The Triune Brain in Evolution; Role of Paleo-cerebral Functions*. Plenum Press, N.Y., 1990.

Madaule, Paul. *When Listening Comes Alive*. Norval, Ontario Moulin Publishing, 1993.

Russell, Ronald. *Using your Whole Brain*. Hampton Roads Publishing Company, Inc, Norfolk, Va., 1993.

Russell, Ronald. *Focusing the Whole Brain*. Hampton Roads Publishing Company, Inc., Charlottesville, Va., 2004.

Tomatis, Dr. Alfred. *The Ear and Language*. Moulin Publishing, Norval, Ontario, 1996.

Appendix D

Music and Metamusic®—A Universal Bridge

Barbara Bullard and Matthew Joyce

I remember being ready to fall asleep as the "special" music began. Ten minutes into the wonderful music, I felt myself lifted out of my body. Soon I soared through the deep blackness of space. Wonder and bliss filled my being as I floated through a vortex of energy. Immediately an awesome melody I can only describe as "music of the spheres" embraced me with transcendent love. My soul overflowed with healing and happiness. Tears of joy streamed down my face. For what seemed a profound eternity I voyaged through the heart of space and music. Eventually I gently floated back into my body on the bed.

Despite years of incorporating music into my meditations and explorations of consciousness, never before had I enjoyed such a rich experience. The power of music helped me transcend the bounds of earth to experience the levels of my soul.[1] To better understand the nature of my experience and the impact of music on our lives, I turned to noted author Wayne Dyer and others who advocate the purposeful use of music for improving our health and gaining greater insights into our lives.

In his book, *You'll See It When You Believe It*, Dyer asks us to consider the word "universe," the term we use to describe the infinite and all-encompassing expanse that surrounds us. Breaking the word into its parts, we see "uni" meaning one and "verse" meaning song. One Song. The entirety of all there is comprises but a single song.

Hidden right there in plain sight is one of the most profound truths of our existence. From ancient Hindu mystics to modern quantum physicists the collective wisdom of humankind has repeatedly discovered that the universe is an immense energy field vibrating on a score of frequencies. No matter how we separate the individual notes, they all play together to create a single harmonious song.[2]

The Bible, so central to the beliefs of many Western cultures, tells us that "In the beginning was the Word." Yet many Eastern and aboriginal cultures maintain that the world was not spoken, but, rather, SUNG into existence. For a growing number of scientists, their research into the impacts of music on the brain and consciousness now favors the influence of song over speech. In fact, quantum string theory describes our bodies, all physical matter, and even the Earth itself, as cosmic instruments staying in tune with a larger universal orchestra.

The night after my first musical epiphany, I gained even more personal experience with this concept. That second evening at The Monroe Institute in Faber, Virginia, I listened to a second "special" composition. This one was more serene, more earthy. Soon after the music started I found myself walking through a lush rain forest. As I strolled among the verdant flora and myriad animals I felt filled with a deep sense of oneness and rapport with Mother Earth. I felt personally compelled to do my part for her healing.

When the experience was over, I asked our group leaders, "What is that special music that's having such an impact on me?" They smiled and told me it was a surprise. The answer would be revealed soon.

The Body-Music Connection

To grasp the widespread impact of music in general, we need only look at the marvelous compilations gathered by the renowned musicologist Don Campbell. His books, *Music and Miracles*, *Music: Physician For Times To Come*, and *The Mozart Effect* cover the spectrum of music's influence on almost every aspect of the listener's body and mind.[3]

Virtually all of us can point to one time or another in our lives when music impacted our emotions. Maybe it was the quiet strains of classical music during a romantic dinner. Perhaps it was toe-tapping rock-n-roll so compelling you just had to dance. Music plays such a central role in our experience that no Hollywood movie dares to do without it. To do so could be box office suicide.

According to Dr. Avram Goldstein of Stanford University, who surveyed people to study the impacts of various emotional stimuli, music was the single most influential factor with a "thrill rating" of 95 percent. Second place was the thrill of sex with less than 80 percent.[4] Because music affects the limbic area of the brain—which influences our feelings, monitors our hormonal systems, and governs our body's ability to seek reward and pleasure in our lives—we can't help but feel the impact of music on our emotions.

But music impacts far more than simply our feelings. It also affects our heart-rate, body metabolism, blood pressure, muscular energy, digestion, circulation, nutrition, fatigue, cholesterol levels, and brain development—just to name a few of the many other bodily elements subject to its influence. "There is scarcely a single function of the body which cannot be affected by musical tones," says author David Tame, in *The Secret Power of Music*.[5]

German jazz theorist Jochim Ernst Berendt had an epiphany with music that was comparable to mine. His inspired him to research all the world's religions to learn how music and sound affect the brain and consciousness. He shared his findings in *The World Is Sound- Nada Brahma*, which devoted special attention to musicians who are composing "new music of transformation."[6] The book became a classic within six months.

Musicians and readers were particularly inspired by his chapter "The Temple in the Ear," which explores the overwhelming importance of the auditory nerve and the influence of music and sound on consciousness and health. In it Berendt points to radiological studies of MRIs which demonstrate that our auditory nerve has three times as many connections to the brain as vision does.

This becomes important for our inner journeys because as composer Murray Schafer states,

"With our eyes we are always at the edge of the world looking in, but with our ears the world comes to us and we are always at the center of it." This is why, he reflects, "Our ears are the organ of transcendence and the gateway to the soul."[7]

Berendt further demonstrates in less esoteric terms how the auditory system also connects to the thymus gland, which is our main regulator in the fight against disease, and thereby influences the immune system. Moreover, says Berendt, the auditory system maintains direct connections to every organ in the body. That means that sounds transmitted through the auditory nerve can heal the body.

"In reality we and the universe are vibration," says Berendt, "and the sound that comes into our brain stimulates not only the brain, but also the entire immune system." That is why Campbell, Berendt and others echo the chorus, Music and mEARicles—Yes!

Because of the strong connection between our auditory nerves, thymus glands and immune systems, certain types of music have proven to be a powerful aid in healing. I experienced this first hand when I later played some of the "special" music for one of my students, Aaron, who was in the hospital dying of AIDS-related complications.

I took three "special" CDs, *Inner Journey*, *Sleeping Through the Rain*, and *Cloudscapes* to the hospital. I left them with Aaron's mother, instructing her to put on the music whenever Aaron needed sleep or relief from pain. Days later on my second visit, I was greeted by a nurse who asked where she could purchase the "miracle music" for the hospice wing. The nurse said that as long as the music was on Aaron needed no morphine.

I went into Aaron's room and quickly learned that this "special" music is something more than ordinary music.

As we talked, the music ended. Within five minutes, I noticed a ripple of pain several inches wide spreading from Aaron's face all the way down to his toes.

"Is the music off?!" he screamed.

"Yes," I said as I restarted the music.

"I told them not to turn it off. It doesn't hurt when the music is on," Aaron told me.

In less than 10 minutes Aaron's pain eased.

Aaron's favorite "special" music was *Sleeping Through The Rain.* He turned to *Inner Journey* to feel closer Oneness with God as he made his final transition.

Should it be surprising that music could have such an impact on Aaron? Or on me? I don't think so. Holistic physician and psychiatrist John Diamond, M.D., explores the relationship between music and health in his book, *The Life Energy in Music.* In it he notes that at some point 95 percent of the population will suffer from low thymus levels and fatigue. This low thymus activity can be instantly raised by listening to enhancing and soothing music that mitigates the effects of everyday stress and noxious stimuli. Diamond suggests that music can increase T-cell production to five times normal levels, raise endorphin levels up to 90 times, improve resistance to illness, dampen the perception of pain, and evoke faster recovery times.[8]

As a further testament to the healing power of music, Dr. Diamond cites findings on the unusual longevity of classical music conductors. "At the age of seventy, by which point 50 percent of American men are deceased, 80 percent of conductors are not only alive, but active and working," he writes in *Your Body Doesn't Lie*. Truly, there is something incredibly therapeutic about music.[9]

Music in Our Genes

Larry Dossey, M.D. reaches a similar conclusion in his excellent article, "The Body as Music." In it Dossey eloquently addresses an even deeper level of music when he states: "Why are we moved by music? One reason may be that the body itself is intrinsically musical, right down to the DNA that makes up our genes."[10]

The idea that DNA and music might be connected originates with the work of Dr. Susumu Ohno, a geneticist at the Beckman Institute of the City of Hope Hospital in Duarte, California. Dr. Ohno has notated more than fifteen songs based on the DNA of a variety of living organisms.

He finds that the more evolved an organism, the more complicated the music. The DNA of a single-cell protozoan, for example, translates into a simple four-note repetition. But music transcribed from human DNA—such as the body's receptor site for insulin—is much more complex.[11]

"Listeners knowledgeable about classical music hear similarities between these DNA-based compositions and the music of Bach, Brahms, Chopin, and other great composers," writes Dr. Ohno. "DNA melodies are majestic and inspiring. Many persons hearing them for the first time are moved to tears. They cannot believe that their bodies, which they believed to be mere collections of chemicals, contain such uplifting, inspiring harmonies—that they are musical."

Not only can one make music starting with DNA, it is also possible to reverse the process. In other words, you take a piece of music and assign nucleotides to the notes. The end result resembles a strand of DNA. Ohno tried this with a Chopin piece and the final result resembled a cancer gene!

Now if music affects us down to the level of DNA, I believe each of our organs is singing its own song. We are healthy when our organs are singing in harmony. We feel sick when they are singing out of tune. From my own experiences it is clear that listening to music helps the body stay in tune.

A Melody a Day Keeps the Doctor Away

For optimal health, Steven Halpern, Ph.D., a foremost creator of healing music, suggests listening to music with an alpha/theta brainwave rhythm (alpha is 7-13 Hertz and theta is 3-7 Hertz) for a minimum of thirty minutes per day.[12] Halpern bases this statement, in part, on an understanding of the correlation between vibrations in the Earth's electromagnetic field and those of the human body. The Earth vibrates at an inaudible frequency of approximately 8 cycles per second. When the human body is deeply relaxed it too vibrates at approximately 8 cycles per second. This sympathetic resonance is known as Schumann's Resonance, and it implies that being in harmony with oneself and the universe may be more than a mere poetic concept.

Listening to alpha and theta frequencies as Halpern describes helps to induce a trophotropic state, a powerful healing condition in the body. The opposite of this state is the ergotropic state, which triggers a fight or flight response that causes stress and fatigue. Hectic schedules and over stimulation naturally force us into ergotropic states that eventually lead to exhaustion, sleep deprivation, and illness. Relaxing and listening to music in the alpha/theta range brings on a trophotropic state and helps restore balance.[13]

Knowing this, the question then becomes, what kind of music supports synchronized alpha/theta brainwave states? Since each of us is unique and has differing needs what feels restful and healing for some may not be appealing to others. However, there are certain desirable qualities in music to be used for inner work. The most appropriate music tends to be the opposite of the kind that we play in our cars and homes as we hustle and bustle through our busy days. More often than not, inner space music contains no vocals since lyrics stimulate the logic-dominant left hemisphere of the brain, as opposed to our more creative right hemispheres. Inner music also tends to feature slower rhythms that help our heart rates and brainwaves to slow down. Furthermore, the musical formats are generally harmonic with instrumentation that facilitates an introspective or contemplative mode. The most effective musical selections are those that permit your mind to wander gently and enter a peaceful state of being. The soundtrack may center on the ambience of nature, which can help you get in tune with the natural environment, or it may feature more ethereal sounds and long moments of silence where some say we can experience Oneness or God.

So where can you find music like this? Fortunately, we live in an era of the synthesizer, new instrumentation, and the internet—all of which provide access to a cornucopia of music conducive for healing and exploring inner realms. The best way to find something suitable is to browse the aisles of your favorite music stores or to surf the web. Some good places online to start include: www.backroadsmusic.com, www.healingmusic.org, and www.ethereanmusic.com. In terms of recording artists, you might want to consider works by Aeoliah, Don Campbell, Dik Darnell, Constance Demby, Steven Halpern, Steve Roach, Jonn Serrie, or Robin Spielberg, to name a few perennial favorites.

However, finding the right music is just the first step. To truly make the most of the listening experience we must also be willing to fully participate in the process by surrendering to the "intent" of the music.

Constance Demby, a well-respected symphonic space musician, whose classic *Novus Magnificat* was voted by New Age Voice as one of the 25 most influential ambient albums of all time, explains that for the music to take you to soul levels you must be a willing participant. She encourages listeners to participate in "frontal listening," as opposed to background listening. Ask to be taken to the same realms that the music came from, she says. Open your heart, surrender, and let the music in all the way. People can go much further when they consciously focus on the music and surrender to it. By allowing their minds to follow the music they are led to the Source of the music—and its transformational power. In a sense, it means meditating with the music.[14]

Therefore, when listening to music for healing or voyages to inner and outer space, it's best to begin with the proper attitude. Next, sit or lie down in a noise-free environment where you know that you will not be disturbed for at least 45 minutes. Make sure that you've rid yourself of all distractions. The best approach is to create a sacred space where you can relax, reduce worrisome thoughts, and minimize external stimuli. Doing so helps to open yourself to inner visions created by the auditory nerve's response to the music.

It's clear to me that I wouldn't have had such profound experiences with music if I had not also been in a conducive state of acceptance. At the Monroe Institute, renowned for facilitating states of expanded consciousness and out-of-body experiences, we were freed from all our daily distractions—no watches, cell phones, newspapers, or TVs—for an entire week. My colleagues and I each came with the intention to explore the consciousness of inner and outer space. I am certain that being in the right frame of mind helped facilitate my transformational musical encounters.

So, what was the "special" music they played for us at the Monroe Institute?

More than Music—Metamusic®

I eventually found out at the concluding morning session of my weeklong professional workshop. The compositions I'd been listening to, and those I later gave to Aaron, were what is called *Metamusic®*. The first evening was titled, *Inner Journey*, and the second evening was *Sleeping Through the Rain*.

Metamusic® is music that is specifically designed to promote healing and encourage voyages to inner and outer space. The audible musical compositions are then significantly enhanced by the synergistic addition of Hemi-Sync® brainwave signals. These subaudible electrical sound wave patterns are blended and sequenced to support different states of consciousness.

Hemi-Sync® works by playing slightly different tones in each ear, which then harmonize inside your brain. To better understand, imagine playing two notes on the piano. If played one after the other you hear the difference between them. But when played at the same time, you hear them in harmony. Hemi-Sync® works the same way, except that since the tones are subaudible the synchronization process occurs inside your brain instead of outside your ear. When precisely controlled Hemi-Sync® tones are combined in the brain, the entire brain begins to resonate. It becomes 'entrained' to the frequency, producing a unique whole-brain state known as hemispheric synchronization, or Hemi-Sync®. When Hemi-Sync® is added to relaxing music the result is Metamusic®.

The magic of Hemi-Sync® and Metamusic® lies in its capacity to deliberately and directly induce the trophotropic state. By recording subaudible alpha and theta frequencies beneath the already engaging music The Monroe Institute creates musical tools with a powerful healing potential.

Many people first seek Metamusic® for meditation, inner exploration, or for guided imagery work. Favorite selections among Monroe Institute enthusiasts include: *Ascension* and *Higher,* both by J.S. Epperson*, Deep Journeys* by Steven Halpern*, Inner Journey* and *The Journey Home,* both by Micah Sadigh, and *Mystic Realms* and *Into the Deep* by Matthew Sigmon and Julie Anderson.

Because the Hemi-Sync® tones can be adjusted to any frequency, including the sleep-inducing delta range, Metamusic® can also be used to help people with insomnia and sleep disruptions. More than 30 million Americans suffer from insomnia and sleep disorders. Metamusic® helps a growing number of them to drift off to sleep more readily and enjoy rapid eye movement (REM) sleep, which is essential for good health. The most popular titles of this type are: *Midsummer Night* by Alan Phillips, *Sleeping Through the Rain* by Matthew Sigmon and Julie Anderson, *Portraits* by Lenore Paxton and Phillip Saidi, *Cloudscapes,* by Ray Dreske, *GAIA* by Richard Roberts, and *Transformation* by Micah Sadigh.

Because these musical selections are specifically designed to take listeners into deep states of relaxation and consciousness, they should NEVER be used while driving a car or moving vehicle.

Metamusic® is not just for inner work and healing though. By combining music with Hemi-Sync® frequencies in the stimulating beta harmonic range, it can be used to induce periods of sustained creative energy and mental concentration. Titles such as *Illumination, Remembrance, Einstein's Dream,* and *Indigo for Quantum Focus*, all by J.S. Epperson, as well as *Seasons at Robert's Mountain* by Scott Bucklin, and *Baroque Garden* by the Arcangelos Chamber Ensemble were all designed to stimulate a coherent brain state that enhances learning and peak performance. Many of selections were created to help those with attention deficit disorder (ADD) and other learning challenges, but they've proven very popular among those who simply want to work and study smarter, not harder.[15]

Conclusion

Music is truly a bridge to good health, and Metamusic® is a marriage between the innate power of music and the wonder of Hemi-Sync®. I agree with Deepak Chopra, M.D.'s belief that it is our duty to humanity to be as healthy as we can possibly be. We are all ripples in a vast cosmic sea, and the vibrations of our mental, physical, and spiritual beings affect everything else. As Chopra says, each of us is, in effect, a wave of sound that hums a tune throughout our lives.[16]

By making conscious choices about the types of music that we listen to we can improve our health, explore inner realms, and enhance our creative and mental performance. As we become healthier and happier through the use of uplifting music, so too do our relationships with others and the world around us. How could it possibly be otherwise when the entire universe is singing a single song?

Appendix D Author:

Matthew Joyce has been exploring human consciousness for more than 20 years. He is the publisher of Higher Self Guides. He writes frequently on self-improvement and metaphysical topics.

Appendix D Endnotes

[1]Wayne Dyer, *You'll See It When You Believe It, p.88*
[2] Lynne McTaggart, *The Field,* Quill Publishing
[3] Don Campbell, *Music and Miracles, Music: Physician For Times To Come,* and *The Mozart Effect*

[4] Avram Goldstein, *Physiological Psychology*, 1980, Vol 8 (1), pp. 126-129

[5] David Tame, *The Secret Power of Music*

[6] Jochim Ernst Berendt, *The World Is Sound- Nada Brahma, Destiny Books and The Third Ear.* Henry Holt & Co

[7] Murray Schafer, *Music Physician for Times to Come*, ed. Don Campbell, p. 74

[8] John Diamond, *The Life Energy in Music*

[9] John Diamond, *Your Body Doesn't Lie*

[10] Larry Dossey, "The Body as Music," *Music and Miracles*, ed. Campbell, pp. 55-56

[11] Ibid. (For more info on DNA Music see www.oursounduniverse.com or www.dnamusic.com.)

[12] Steven Halpern, www.spiritinthesmokies.com/interview

[13] Alan Hobson, M.D. "Sleep and the Immune System," *The Chemistry of Conscious States: How the Brain Changes Its Mind*

[14] Constance Demby, www.newagevoice.com

[15] For more info on the beta-Metamusic® read *Focusing The Whole Brain*, ed. Russell, Hampton Roads or RemembranceMusic.com for "Metamusic®: Opening The Learning Door in the ADD Mind, *Children of the New Earth*, Vol. 2, Issue 2

[16] Deepak Chopra, M.D., "Music and Vibrational Healing," *Yoga Journal*, March/April 1993, p. 109

Index

About the Authors

Barbara Bullard, M.A., has worked as a Professor of Speech Communications at Orange Coast College for over 46 years. During her tenure at OCC, she has won numerous awards, most notably among them the NISOD Teaching Excellence Award (1994, 1999, 2000, 2002, and 2003), was written up in the publication "Who's Who in America's Teachers" (2002-present), and honored with OCC's Faculty Member of the Year nomination seven times since 1994. She is the co-author of *Communication from the Inside Out.*

Professor Bullards's work as a teacher and her years as a parent raising two children with Attention Deficit Disorder led her to become very interested in music as a universal means by which her students and children could overcome their learning challenges, improve their learning abilities, and heighten their performance in the educational setting. This interest eventually led Bullard to work with the Professional Division of The Monroe Institute—where she was exposed to decades of research on the brain and how frequencies can be used as a tool for healing the body and mind, as well as the fruits of that research: Hemi-Sync®.

Her fascination with the amazing results of Hemi-Sync® led to Professor Bullard's collaboration with the Monroe Institute marrying musical formats with the binaural technology of Hemi-Sync®, now known as Metamusic®. Over the past 20 years, the collaborative result, ***Remembrance***, has proven to be extraordinarily helpful for the normative student as well as those with a variety of learning challenges—specifically ADD, ADHD, and Dyslexia.

Metamusic®, which combines appropriate musical formats with patented Hemi-Sync®, is a type of "designer music," designed to facilitate whole-brained Beta brainwave states necessary for quantum learning. Professor Bullard's other collaborations with the Monroe Institute include *Einstein's Dream*, *Seasons at Robert's Mountain, Indigo for Quantum Focus*, and most recently *Illuminations*, *Lightfall, Breakthrough, and Revelations For Heightened Creativity*, *Guitara Classica, Golden Mind, Elation*

Professor Barbara Bullard is an internationally recognized lecturer known for her inspiring and informative style. As an expert on the brain, mind, and body—she is asked to speak regularly at conventions across the world, and has been a featured expert on videos promoting Super-learning. As the owner of Remembrance Music and Quantum Technologies, she regularly promotes the uses and benefits of Metamusic®. Due to her innovative work in the field of education and her efforts with the Monroe Institute, she is a much sought-after speaker.

As a Speaker ...

"Barbara's delivery is humorous and challenging. She received a standing ovation for her inspirational message on healing our primary relationships and on her work with the Monroe Institute, which help us bridge to the 21st Century!"—**Pat Rosenblad, TX**

"Her presentation? Splendid! Her delivery? Awesome!"—**Clara Pascar, Sequin, TX**

"A memorable experience that I hope others can share."—**Neil Powell, Austin, TX**

"We met in Ft. Myers in January 1996--changed my life!"—**Theresa Dearduff, FL** "...The insights I have gained due to the facilitation of our class and your love has been invaluable to me!" —**David J., CA**

"Barbara keeps her audience enthralled and at the same time engulfed with laughter, for she sees the humor in the human scene. [She is] one of the best teachers to come down the pike in decades."—**Jim Dixon, VA**

Barbara may be reached at BrainSync@aol.com
Related websites are: www.dnamusic.com and www.remembrancemusic.com
Barbara on You Tube: www.**youtube**.com/user/Prof**BarbaraBullard**

Alex Bennet, Ph.D., is the former Chief Knowledge Officer and Deputy Chief Information Officer of the U.S. Department of the Navy. She simultaneously served as Co-Chair of the Federal Knowledge Management Working Group, acting as internal consultant across the U.S. Federal sector, and previously served as the Acquisition Reform Officer and Standards Improvement Executive. She is the recipient of both Distinguished and Superior Public Service Awards from the U.S. government.

Alex is co-founder, with her partner Dr. David Bennet, of the **Mountain Quest Institute** (MQI), a research and retreat center nestled in the Allegheny Mountains of West Virginia dedicated to helping individuals achieve personal and professional growth and organizations create and sustain high performance in a rapidly changing, uncertain, and increasingly complex world. MQI is scientific, humanistic and spiritual and finds no contradiction in this combination. The Bennets travel around the world speaking, and facilitate workshops and off-sites in the MQI retreat center.

The Drs. Bennet publish extensively, combining new findings in neuroscience with knowledge, systems and complexity theory with a focus on sustainable high performance in a CUCA world (increasing Change, Uncertainty, Complexity and Anxiety). They are co-authors of the seminal work, *Organizational Survival in the New World: The Intelligent Complex Adaptive System* (Elsevier, 2004), a new theory of the firm that enables an organization to co-evolve with its environment. More recently they worked with the Social Science and Humanities Research Council of Canada to write and publish *Knowledge Mobilization in the Social Sciences and Humanities: Moving from Research to Action* (MQIPress, 2007). (Both are available in hardback and as eBooks.) Additional books published through MQIPress include: *The Course of Knowledge: A 21ˢᵗ Century Theory*; *Expanding the Self: The Intelligent Complex Adaptive Learning System*; *Decision-Making in The New Reality: Complexity, Knowledge and Knowing*; and *Leading with the Future in Mind: Knowledge and Emergent Leadership*. More recently The Bennets collaborated with researchers Dr. Arthur Shelley, Dr. Theresa Bullard, Dr. John Lewis and Dr. Donna Panucci to develop and publish the five-book series titled The Profundity and Bifurcation of Change, laying the groundwork for the Intelligent Social Change Journey, a developmental journey of the body, mind and heart in which we are engage. Grounded in this series, Alex developed 22 little Conscious Look Books called *Possibilities that are YOU!* These books are conversational in nature which are geared toward the graduate of life experience, helping us to more fully become the co-creators that we are.

In their ever-expanding exploration of the Cosmos, the Bennets have published two eBooks in their *Myst* series, both available from Amazon. The first is *The Journey into the Myst*, an amazing adventure that begins with a miracle and continues taking them into uncharted territory. The second is *Patterns in the Myst*. This volume brings Science into the spiritual experience, bringing to bear what the Bennets have learned through their research and educational experiences. Embracing the paralogical, patterns in the *Myst* are observed, felt, interpreted, analyzed and compared in terms of their physical make-up, non-randomness, intelligent sources and potential implications.

Alex has degrees in Human and Organizational Systems, Human Development, Management for Organizational Effectiveness, English and Marketing. Dr. Bennet is affiliated with several Universities in the US, is a Professor at Bangkok University Institute for Knowledge and Innovation Management, mentors at Erasmus University Rotterdam Management School, is a member of the Profession Division of The Monroe Institute, and serves on the International Advisory Board of the World Capital Institute.

Alex can be contacted at alex@mountainquestinstitute.com
Related websites are: www.mountainquestinstitute.com www.mountainquestinn.com and www.Myst-Art.com

MQIPress is a wholly-owned subsidiary of Mountain Quest Institute, LLC., located at 303 Mountain Quest Lane, Marlinton, West Virginia, 24954, USA.

Other Books by These Authors

Possibilities that are YOU!

by Alex Bennet. These little **Conscious Look Books** are focused on sharing 22 large concepts from *The Profundity and Bifurcation of Change.* Conversational in nature, each with seven ideas offered for the graduate of life experience. These little books include: *Transcendent Beauty, Grounding, Engaging Forces, Conscious Compassion, Truth in context, Intention and Attention, Living Virtues for Today, ME as Co-Creator, connections as Patterns, Knowing, All Things in Balance, The Emerging Self, The ERC's of Intuition, The Emoting Guidance System, Seeking Wisdom, Associative Patterning and Attracting, The Creative Leap, Staying on the Path, The Art of Thought Adjusting, the Humanness of Humility, The Bifurcation,* and *Beyond Action.* Available in soft cover from Amazon.

The Intelligent Social Change Journey

These little **Conscious Look Books** are focused on sharing 22 large concepts from *The Profundity and Bifurcation of Change*.

eBooks available in PDF format from MQIPress (US 304-799-7267 or alex@mountainquestinstitute.com) and Kindle format from Amazon. (Soft cover copies available 2020)

Five in-depth eBooks, *The Profundity and Bifurcation of Change*, heavily referenced and resourced. These books lay the groundwork for the **Intelligent Social Change Journey** (ISCJ), a developmental journey of the body, mind and heart, moving from the heaviness of cause-and-effect linear extrapolations, to the fluidity of co-evolving with our environment, to the lightness of breathing our thought and feelings into reality. Grounded in development of our mental faculties, these are phase changes, each building on and expanding previous learning in our movement toward intelligent activity. Available as eBooks from Amazon. (Available 2019 in soft cover.)

Other Books by MQI Press

Other Books available from in softback and Kindle formats from Amazon.

The Course of Knowledge: A 21st Century Theory
by Alex Bennet and David Bennet with Joyce Avedisian (2015)
Knowledge is at the core of what it is to be human, the substance which informs our thoughts and determines the course of our actions. Our growing focus on, and understanding of, knowledge and its

consequent actions is changing our relationship with the world. Because **knowledge determines the quality of every single decision we make**, it is critical to learn about and understand what knowledge is. **From a 21st century viewpoint,** we explore a theory of knowledge that is both pragmatic and biological. Pragmatic in that it is based on taking effective action, and biological because it is created by humans via patterns of neuronal connections in the mind/brain.

In this book we explore *the course of knowledge*. Just as a winding stream in the bowls of the mountains curves and dips through ravines and high valleys, so, too, with knowledge. In a continuous journey towards intelligent activity, context-sensitive and situation-dependent knowledge, imperfect and incomplete, experientially engages a changing landscape in a continuous cycle of learning and expanding. *We are in a continuous cycle of knowledge creation such that every moment offers the opportunity for the emergence of new and exciting ideas, all waiting to be put in service to an interconnected world.* Learn more about this **exciting human capacity**!

Expanding the Self: The Intelligent Complex Adaptive Learning System
by David Bennet, Alex Bennet and Robert Turner (2015)

We live in unprecedented times; indeed, turbulent times that can arguably be defined as ushering humanity into a new Golden Age, offering the opportunity to embrace new ways of learning and living in a globally and collaboratively entangled connectedness (Bennet & Bennet, 2007). In this shifting and dynamic environment, life demands accelerated cycles of learning experiences. Fortunately, we as a humanity have begun to look within ourselves to better understand the way our mind/brain operates, the amazing qualities of the body that power our thoughts and feelings, and the reciprocal loops as those thoughts and feelings change our physical structure. This emerging knowledge begs us to relook and rethink what we know about learning, providing a new starting point to expand toward the future.

This book is a treasure for those interested in how recent findings in neuroscience impact learning. The result of this work is an expanding experiential learning model called the Intelligent Complex Adaptive Learning System, adding the fifth mode of social engagement to Kolb's concrete experience, reflective observation, abstract conceptualization and active experimentation, with the five modes undergirded by the power of Self. A significant conclusion is that should they desire, adults have much more control over their learning than they may realize.

Decision-Making in The New Reality: Complexity, Knowledge and Knowing
by Alex Bennet and David Bennet (2013)

We live in a world that offers many possible futures. The ever-expanding complexity of information and knowledge provide many choices for decision-makers, and we are all making decisions every single day! As the problems and messes of the world become more complex, our decision consequences are more and more difficult to anticipate, and our decision-making processes must change to keep up with this world complexification. This book takes a consilience approach to explore decision-making in The New Reality, fully engaging systems and complexity theory, knowledge research, and recent neuroscience findings. It also presents methodologies for decision-makers to tap into their unconscious, accessing tacit knowledge resources and increasingly relying on the sense of knowing that is available to each of us.

Almost every day new energies are erupting around the world: new thoughts, new feelings, new knowing, all contributing to new situations that require new decisions and actions from each and every one of us. Indeed, with the rise of the Net Generation and social media, a global consciousness may well be emerging. As individuals and organizations we are realizing that there are larger resources available to us, and that, as complex adaptive systems linked to a flowing fount of knowing, we can bring these resources to bear to achieve our ever-expanding vision of the future. Are we up to the challenge?

Leading with the Future in Mind: Knowledge and Emergent Leadership
by Alex Bennet and David Bennet with John Lewis (2015)

We exist in a new reality, a global world where the individuated power of the mind/brain offers possibilities beyond our imagination. It is within this framework that thought leading emerges, and when married to our collaborative nature, makes the impossible an everyday occurrence. *Leading with the Future in Mind*, building on profound insights unleashed by recent findings in neuroscience, provides a new view that converges leadership, knowledge and learning for individual and organizational advancement.

This book provides a research-based *tour de force* for the future of leadership. Moving from the leadership of the past, for the few at the top, using authority as the explanation, we now find leadership emerging from all levels of the organization, with knowledge as the explanation. The future will be owned by the organizations that can master the relationships between knowledge and leadership. Being familiar with the role of a knowledge worker is not the same as understanding the role of a knowledge leader. As the key ingredient, collaboration is much more than "getting along"; it embraces and engages. Wrapped in the mantle of collaboration and engaging our full resources—hysical, mental, emotional and spiritual—we open the door to possibilities. We are dreaming the future together.

Also available in Kindle format from Amazon.

REMEMBRANCE: Pathways to Expanded Learning with Music and Metamusic® (as eBook)
by Barbara Bullard and Alex Bennet (2013)

Take a journey of discovery into the last great frontier—the human mind/brain, an instrument of amazing flexibility and plasticity. This eBook is written for brain users who are intent on mining more of the golden possibilities that lie inherent in each of our unique brains. Begin by discovering the role positive attitudes play in learning, and the power of self affirmations and visualizations. Then explore the use of brain wave entrainment mixed with designer music called Metamusic® to achieve enhanced learning states. Join students of all ages who are creating magical learning outcomes using music and Metamusic.®

The Journey into the Myst (Vol 1 of The Myst Series)
by Alex Bennet and David Bennet (2012)

What we are about to tell you would have been quite unbelievable to me before this journey began. It is not a story of the reality either of us has known for well over our 60 and 70 years of age, but rather, the reality of dreams and fairytales." This is the true story of a sequence of events that happened at Mountain Quest Institute, situated in a high valley of the Allegheny Mountains of West Virginia. The story begins with a miracle, expanding into the capture and cataloging of thousands of pictures of electromagnetic spheres widely known as "orbs." This joyous experience became an exploration into the unknown with the emergence of what the author's fondly call the Myst, the forming and shaping of non-random patterns such as human faces, angels and animals. As this phenomenon unfolds, you will discover how the Drs. Alex and David Bennet began to observe and interact with the Myst. This book shares the beginning of an extraordinary *Journey into the Myst*. AVAILABLE as an eBook FROM AMAZON and in 2020 with soft-back cover.

Patterns in the Myst (Vol 2 of The Myst Series)

    by Alex Bennet and David Bennet (2013)

The Journey into the Myst was just the beginning for Drs. Alex and David Bennet. Volume II of the Myst Series brings Science into the Spiritual experience, bringing to bear what the Bennets have learned through their research and educational experiences in physics, neuroscience, human systems, knowledge management and human development. Embracing the paralogical, patterns in the Myst are observed, felt, interpreted, analyzed and compared in terms of their physical make-up, non-randomness, intelligent sources and potential implications. Along the way, the Bennets were provided amazing pictures reflecting the forming of the Myst. The Bennets shift to introspection in the third volume of the series to explore the continuing impact of the Myst experience on the human psyche. AVAILABLE as an eBook FROM AMAZON and in 2020 with soft-back cover.

CPSIA information can be obtained
at www.ICGtesting.com
Printed in the USA
LVHW061305070622
720690LV00016B/173